THE LIFE OF THE MIND

RenewedMinds

RenewedMinds, an imprint of
Baker Academic in partnership
with the Council for Christian
Colleges & Universities, pub-
lishes quality textbooks and
academic resources to guide
readers in reflecting critically
on contemporary issues of faith
and learning. While focused on
the needs of a Christian higher-
education curriculum,
RenewedMinds resources will
engage and benefit all thoughtful readers.

The Council for Christian Colleges & Universities is an association of
more than ninety-five member colleges and universities, each of which
has a curriculum rooted in the arts and sciences and is committed to
the integration of biblical faith, scholarship, and service. More than
thirty Christian denominations, committed to a variety of theological
traditions and perspectives, are represented by these member institutions. The views expressed in these volumes are primarily those of the
author(s) and are not intended to serve as a position statement of the
Council membership.

For more information, please use one of the following addresses:

www.cccu.org

council@cccu.org

The Council for Christian Colleges & Universities
321 Eighth Street N.E.
Washington, D.C. 20002-6518

THE LIFE OF THE MIND

A CHRISTIAN PERSPECTIVE

CLIFFORD WILLIAMS

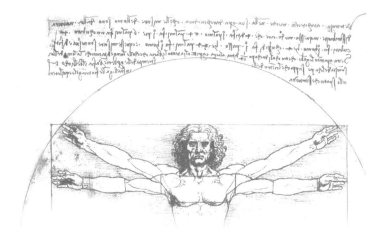

A RenewedMinds Book

Baker Academic

A Division of Baker Book House Co
Grand Rapids, Michigan 49516

Published by Baker Academic
a division of Baker Book House Company
P.O. Box 6287, Grand Rapids, MI 49516-6287

Second printing, October 2002

Printed in the United States of America

Library of Congress Cataloging-in-Publication Data

Williams, Clifford, 1943–
    The life of the mind : a Christian perspective / Clifford Williams.
       p.   cm.
    Includes bibliographical references.
    ISBN 0-8010-2336-X (pbk.)
    1. Faith and reason—Christianity. 2. Christians—Intellectual
life. I. Title.
BT50.W475 2002
261.5—dc21   2001043377

Scripture quotations are from the New Revised Standard Version of the Bible,
copyright 1989 by the Division of Christian Education of the National Council of the Churches of Christ in the USA. Used by permission.

For information about Baker Academic, visit our web site:
www.bakerbooks.com/academic

Our danger has not been too much thinking, but not enough.

NATHAN HATCH

CONTENTS

PREFACE

CHRISTIANS HAVE MIXED FEELINGS about purely intellectual pursuits. On the one hand, many believe that thinking
and learning can enrich faith and devotion. Those who believe
this support Christian colleges and want to see a higher intellectual level among Christians.

Other Christians, however, are suspicious of too much thinking and learning and even more so of a life devoted to them. Those
who hold this opinion are convinced not only that thinking and
learning are useless to faith and devotion but that they are likely
to undermine faith and devotion. To these Christians, being a
thinker does not comport well with being a Christian.

But is the life of the mind at odds with Christian faith? Let's
begin this discussion by examining characteristics of faith that
appear to be in tension with intellectual pursuits.

One of the most evident characteristics of faith is that it is stable and enduring. It does not change with passing whims, intellectual fads, or the advent of new theories. It remains steady
through personal trials and cultural deterioration. It has the innocence and directness of a child's trust in her parents. In addition,
faith focuses on one object: God. It does not go off in different
directions, pursuing one then another object of devotion.

Thinkers, though, have drives that do not fit well with these
characteristics of faith. They are impulsively inquisitive, which
means they go wherever the paths they are on take them. They
do not like to stay in one spot; doing so would be stagnation and

intellectual death. Their inquisitiveness makes them restless, curious to find something new. When they come to the end of an inquiry, they hold the beliefs they have acquired with varying degrees of tentativeness. Though they are confident about some of them, they are willing to give up others should a further consideration come to light. It seems difficult, then, for the inquisitive person to have stable trust or unwandering devotion to God. There may be no logical inconsistency between thinking and faith, but each has an ethos that is alien to the other.

Thinkers are also imaginative. They create new possibilities and ask, "What if . . . ?" "What if we looked at the matter from a different angle?" "What if we let go of that assumption?" They are not content to accept the old just because it is old. They want to discover new perspectives.

Christianity, however, is an orthodoxy. To be a Christian is to accept long-established doctrines, which means that those who are inventive and innovative may feel constricted. This is true of any system of beliefs that has a history, such as Marxism or Freudianism. An imaginative person may experience a fair amount of unease in any of these settings.

There is also a social angle to the tension between imaginativeness and Christianity. A chief feature of nearly every group of people is pressure to conform to the standards and expectations of the group. Without conformity, the cohesiveness of the group is lost, and individuals in the group feel disconnected from each other.

The imaginative person, however, is not bound by pressure to conform. Her imaginativeness continually resists this pressure. She becomes wary of others in a cohesive group and acts with reserve and caution. Others become uncomfortable in her presence, if not outrightly suspicious. Again, two alien sentiments emerge.

These sentiments become especially intense when the pressure to conform takes on a conscious authoritarian air. In such an atmosphere, one is overtly expected to believe what the group believes or what a leader of the group declares. The natural consequence of this condition is that intellectual exploration and thinking for oneself are cowed. One cannot be inquisitive or imaginative without risking not just suspicion but ostracism.

Christian churches and colleges are not immune to the pressure to conform or to an authoritarian air. It sometimes seems, in fact, as if institutional Christianity prizes conformity and engenders authoritarian individuals. Since the very identity of a Christian assemblage is threatened if its members are not Christian, conforming to certain standards becomes essential. This creates a breeding ground for exercising authority and public disapproval. It is difficult to imagine thinking Christians remaining long in such a condition.

Faith possesses two other characteristics that may create tension with genuine thinking. One is its apparent disconnection with reason, and the other is its direct experiential nature. Many Christians think faith goes beyond reason. In other words, faith is not the sort of thing for which evidence can be given. If evidence for it could be given, it would not be faith but knowledge. Faith has no rational foundation, these Christians say; it is a direct and personal experience of the living God.

Not all Christians think of faith in these ways, to be sure, but those who do are less likely to value thinking, at least with respect to faith itself. They may respect the use of reason in other arenas, but if they believe that reason cannot touch faith, then they will resist applying it to faith. Doing so would undermine faith's direct, experiential nature and turn it into impersonal concepts.

A further source of tension between intellectual pursuits and Christian faith is the conviction that intellectual activity is unimportant compared to living the Christian life. If loving God is central to the Christian life, then poking around in libraries or laboratories pales in comparison. And if developing Christian virtues is of paramount importance, we need to interact with others, not just bury ourselves in books. The same tension results from the belief that focusing our attention on God and on the ways of God has eternal significance, whereas directing our concerns to creaturely affairs has only temporal significance. Clearly, we should concentrate on the former and not on the latter.

Central, too, to Christianity is the division between those who align themselves with Christianity and those who do not, between the saved and the unsaved, the sheep and the goats. This theme gives rise to an "us versus them" mentality. "We" are good and "they" are not; "we" are in God's favor and "they" are not. Frequently, the "they" are intellectuals: professors who ridicule the faith of their students, biologists who promulgate evolution, authors who have little awareness of Christian values, judges who rule without regard for historic Christian standards, and academics who

11

promulgate postmodernism, relativism, and unbridled freedom. Due to these considerations, numerous Christians distrust the intellectual life. It is too dangerous, and it is corrupting.

Other Christians, though, believe that imagination and inquisitiveness are given to us by God. Deliberately refraining from using these gifts, therefore, is like burying our talents. Still other Christians support Christian higher education because they see its extensive benefits to individual Christians. Christians need to be prepared for the marketplace. They need to be able to witness to others in the culture, which they cannot do unless they understand it. They need to be able to defend their faith. Young Christians need to be protected against the corruptions of a secular academic environment. They need to be empowered to transform the society in which they will soon become active participants.

On the whole, then, Christians have both distrusted and embraced thinking in general and academia in particular. But even though deep tensions exist between faith and thinking, there are compelling reasons for people of faith to be thinkers. First, thinking and learning affect our character in distinctive ways, and second, these activities have intrinsic value.

This view differs from most Christian defenses of involvement in higher education, which focus largely on fulfilling more practical needs. It focuses, instead, on how Christian learning shapes our character and on the claim that learning is good in and of itself. This approach, as a rationale for Christian higher education, appeals not only to vocational preparation or to transforming secular culture. As such, it is an answer to the question, Why should Christians study things that have little bearing on their future jobs or that do not aim to make them good witnesses to their faith? This approach also explains how learning can invigorate one's Christian life. Understood in this way, it is an invitation to lifelong thinking and reflecting.

The Life of the Mind is intended for several kinds of readers. It is aimed at college students who are wondering about the point of college. It is also aimed at those who are not wondering. This second category is probably much larger than the first, for most students go to college because they are expected to. That, at any rate, is why I went. When I entered college, I had little idea what education is, and it did not occur to me to ask about it. It was only after some of my teachers raised the issue that a few thoughts took root. What I want to do, then, is spur readers to ask themselves why they should value learning.

This book is also aimed at those who, whether they are in or out of college, simply want to reflect on a special feature of the Christian life. One does not have to be in college or to have gone to college to be a thinking Christian.

Finally, the book is intended for people in a wide array of disciplines. I include the full spectrum of arts and sciences in the life of the mind. While some of what I say applies to some parts of the spectrum more than to others, most of what I say is pertinent to the entire spectrum.

ACKNOWLEDGMENTS

I WANT TO THANK Trinity College for the sabbatical during which the pamphlet that was the predecessor to this book was written and for the reduced load grant during the semester I finished the book. I also thank Bob Hosack, Senior Acquisitions Editor at Baker, for suggesting I expand the pamphlet into a book; Viorel Clintoc, Danielle DuBois, Sarah Fowler, Steve Pointer, Michael Sharrow, Joyce Shelton, and Tom Wetzel, for reading and commenting on the manuscript; and Arthur Holmes, for his vision of Christian learning, which he has enunciated on various occasions.

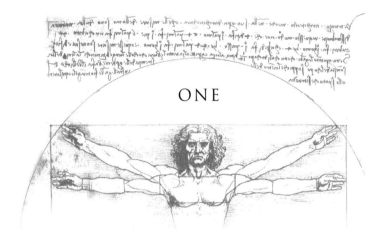

ONE

WHY DO WE LIKE TO THINK?

PEOPLE WHO ENGAGE in the life of the mind—those who think and learn—read, visit libraries, buy books, explore new topics, talk to others about what they are thinking, listen to lectures, and join discussion groups. They like ideas. And they like talking about ideas. What fascinates them is a new discovery, an old classic, the thoughts of an astute observer of human nature, or research into how things work. They like to learn, and they like being with others who like to learn.

Christians who think and learn participate in these same activities and have these same interests. They, too, read and explore. They want knowledge, both of topics that are directly connected to Christian concerns and those that are not. And they like talking with others about what they learn. If you were to ask them what their life passions are, they would mention reading, thinking, and talking about ideas, including Christian ideas.

Of course, these Christians have other life passions as well, and they pursue many other interests besides reading and talking about ideas. Nor is their entire identity wrapped up in books. As far as they are able, they live a balanced life. One part of that life, though, is a fervor for matters of the mind, which is evident in their conversations, their spare-time activities, and the way they approach life as a whole.

Why do they have this fervor? Why do people like to think and learn? A number of motivations lie behind the life of the mind, many of which go beyond the desire to obtain skills and to enhance job prospects.

KNOWING THE WAY THINGS ARE

"Everything holds treasures," A. G. Sertillanges declared, and those who engage in the life of the mind want to find these treasures.[1] They want to know how things work and why things happen as they do. They are endlessly curious about patterns of activity in nature, society, and their own bodies. It is not enough for them to eat, sleep, and work; they must also know.

Imagine a child who is out for a walk with his parents. They are strolling casually through their neighborhood. Sometimes the child lingers behind, glancing at small objects that lie beside the sidewalk. Sometimes he darts ahead, as if to explore uncharted territory. Then he stops at a tree that stands between the sidewalk and the street. He looks up into the tree, then inspects the ground at its base. There he finds a rock, and in an instant he tries to turn it over. He cannot. His look of anguish prompts his mother to reach for the rock. The two hands, one big and one little, turn over the rock together.

Underneath are little crawling things. The child surveys them with delight. He tries to pick one up, his mother scarcely stifling a reprimand. The child rubs his hand along the pockmarked dirt where the rock had lain, then does the same to the bottom and sides of the rock. Before leaving, the same two hands replace the rock.

Those who like to think and learn hunt for new objects to turn over and look under. They cannot imagine themselves not doing so. Their passion for knowledge matches the ceaseless energy of

16

a child who darts to and fro on a sidewalk. They feel restless when weeks pass and they do not encounter a fresh insight into the workings of life and nature.

Those who find astronomy engaging illustrate these points. Like the darting child who finds it fascinating to discover small bugs and big bugs, short ones and long ones, these people are excited about learning that some galaxies are spiral and some elliptical, that of the spiral ones, some are tightly wound and some are loosely wound. Both bugs and galaxies contain treasures that those who like to explore exult in finding.

MAKING BELIEFS COHERENT

We do not like our beliefs to contradict each other. If we suspect that they do, we feel unsettled and try to figure out how to reconcile them. When someone claims we are being inconsistent, we try to show that we are not. When we cannot do so, we give up one of the offending beliefs or set the matter aside for later consideration. The one thing we do not say is, "Contradictions do not bother me. I willingly embrace them."

I am not here referring to paradoxical truths—statements that appear to contradict each other but in fact complement each other, such as, "People are intractably selfish" and "Everyone possesses moral beauty." Nor am I referring to oppositions that dissolve when they are properly qualified, such as Solomon's declarations in Ecclesiastes: "All is vanity" (1:2) and "Fear God, and keep his commandments; for that is the whole duty of everyone" (12:13). I am referring to statements that cannot both be true and cannot both be false, such as, "A loving God would not allow gratuitous torture" and "A loving God would allow gratuitous torture." It is pairs of statements such as these that we cannot accommodate in our belief systems.

In addition to consistency, we also want our beliefs to be unified, that is, to be focused on a central idea. We do not like jumbles, either in our rooms or in our minds. We like to weave our thoughts around a central theme, exhibiting to ourselves how they hang together. When we encounter a new idea that does not quite fit with our current stock of beliefs, we are uneasy until we get it to fit.

17

These two desires—for consistency and for unity—are what constitute the desire for coherence. Christians who like to think and learn possess this desire to an especially high degree. They want to avoid inconsistencies that seep into their thinking due to immersion in a secular culture. And they want to connect what they know to the basic truths of Christianity—that God created everything, that humans have sinned against God, and that God has provided a way to be redeemed from sin. They do not want to be schizophrenic in their thinking; rather, they want their whole mind to revolve around their Christian beliefs.

This drive for coherence is what motivates one to form a worldview. A worldview is a set of concepts that assembles everything else we believe into a coherent whole. This set of concepts constitutes the glasses through which we see life. All that we observe or take in comes through these glasses, unifying everything around a dominant idea. This dominant idea is, in a way, one's primary stance in life—the rock-bottom perspective one takes toward life as a whole.

Consider, as an example, the claim that we possess an unconscious mind containing thoughts, motives, and desires of which we are not aware. This idea surfaced now and then before the twentieth century, but it was Sigmund Freud in the early part of that century who brought it to prominence. Perhaps it was because Freud, an avowed atheist, made so much of it that Christians have not easily embraced it. Yet there is good evidence for the existence of an unconscious mind, evidence that does not depend on atheism for its force. Unless Christians have even stronger reasons to reject the evidence, therefore, those in whom the desire for coherence is prominent will want to come to grips with the claim.

Doing this, unfortunately, is not easy. For one thing, there is the question of how much influence unconscious motives have on our actions. Though there are numerous indications that unconscious motives play a large role in our lives, Christians may be troubled with the loss of responsibility that this appears to entail. For another thing, there is the question of whether unconscious motives are always harmful or sinful. Freudian psychology, with its concepts of unconscious defense mechanisms and repression of painful memories, suggests that they are always troublesome. Christians, though, may want to entertain the hypothesis that God works in our lives through positive unconscious desires.

Because of these uncertainties, it is tempting simply to let the idea of unconscious influence exist side by side in our minds with our Christian beliefs without attempting an accord. Doing this, though, is likely to bring about a bit of consternation from time to time. This disturbing feeling, unfortunately, may well be one of the prices that those who desire coherence have to pay. In any case, they will attempt to work the idea into their worldview, even if they are not entirely sure how to do so.

Consider another example: the big bang theory. This theory states that the universe originated with an explosion of unimaginable speed from an extraordinarily hot and dense mass, "an undifferentiated soup of matter and radiation."[2] As the universe expanded and cooled, atoms formed, then molecules, and much later galaxies and solar systems. The big bang theory is made plausible by two independent discoveries made in the last half of the twentieth century. First, stars and galaxies are moving away from each other at specifiable speeds, which is inferable from the "red shift" in the light spectrum of distant stars and galaxies. Second, there is a cosmic background radiation with a temperature of roughly $3°K$ (Kelvin), which is just a bit above absolute zero. This background radiation appears to be left over from the original explosion, and the cool temperature (roughly $3°K$) is what one would expect from an initial temperature of more than 100,000 million degrees K and years of cooling. Nearly all astrophysicists now regard the big bang theory as the likeliest account of the origin of the universe.[3]

The first reaction Christians should have to the big bang theory is that, if it is true, it describes something that God did. A central tenet of Christianity is that God is Creator of the physical universe; therefore, if the universe began with a massive explosion, then God is responsible for it. Beyond this, however, there is some flexibility. The big bang theory does not say whether the explosion was the very first event in the history of the universe or whether it was preceded by a cosmic implosion. Both of these possibilities are consistent with the theory and with the Christian claim that God is Creator. If the explosion were the first event, then Christians, in order to harmonize the big bang theory with the doctrine of creation *ex nihilo,* would say that at that point God created everything out of nothing. If the explosion were the result of a prior implosion, then Christians would say that the explosion was an instance of God's continuing creative activity. Either way, coherence is achieved.

19

OBTAINING SELF-KNOWLEDGE

What would it be like to go through one's entire life without trying to understand much about who one is? Many do, no doubt. But they are suppressing a fundamental human impulse. If we are sensitive to that impulse, we will acknowledge that we desire to explore a range of concerns about ourselves. We desire to know what kinds of emotions we have and whether they or reason rule us. We want to know how we fit together with others in social structures and how we have gotten to our present stage of history. We want to know about abnormalities, gender differences, ultimate cravings, and the sources of depression. We want to sort through our own desires and find out why we feel as we do.

Christians have these same inclinations, but they also want to know about specifically Christian concerns, such as faith and doubt, forgiveness and guilt, grace and self-justification. Christians want to explore the psychological changes that take place as one's faith matures. They desire to know how guilt and forgiveness affect personality traits. They investigate ways in which self-justification undermines openness to grace. They wonder whether their faith is real or counterfeit.

Because of these proclivities, Christians often find a number of books dealing with matters of the self to be fertile stimulants to self-knowledge. Blaise Pascal's *Pensées,* for example, contains a gold mine of insights about the human condition. His account of diversion reveals the extent to which we go to avoid meeting head-on life's most significant issues. Our days are filled with "hustle and bustle," he declares; we would rather be moving than alone and quiet, for then we become aware of our ulterior motives and misdirected cravings, which we desperately do not want to do. Augustine's *Confessions* is similarly insightful. In book VIII of the *Confessions,* he describes the process by which a choice to sin becomes a habit, which then develops into an addiction that binds us as strongly as iron chains. He depicts the way in which we are caught between these chains and our desire to be free from them. Augustine himself agonized over this dividedness, praying at one point about the lust that bound him, "Give me chastity, but not yet."

In fiction, too, Christians encounter fruitful material for exploring the self. Fyodor Dostoyevsky's *Crime and Punishment* artfully draws the reader into identifying with Raskalnikov's murderous impulse, then with his fluctuation between self-justifying indifference and debilitating guilt. Lastly, the reader is compelled to identify with Raskalnikov's rapturous release from tortured emotions when he at last is able to receive the love of Sonya, a prostitute—and Christ figure—who accepts Raskalnikov despite his ruin. In *The Death of Ivan Ilych,* Leo Tolstoy presents a remarkably picturesque account of the horror of a Russian judge who wriggles and writhes in light of his impending death. Tolstoy displays the sharp disparity between tragedy and beauty by contrasting the agony of the judge with the warm and open response of the judge's servant to the judge.

Christians are drawn not only to individual self-knowledge but to social and cultural self-knowledge as well, for we are social creatures. We want to know how we interact with others in our own culture, how those in other cultures connect with each other, and how people of one gender or race act toward those of another gender or race. Two particularly poignant examples that illuminate the last category are the slave narratives of the nineteenth century and the black protest literature of the early twentieth century. One of the former, *The Life and Times of Frederick Douglass,* vividly depicts the sentiments slaves had toward their owners and the subterfuges in which they engaged to maintain their dignity. Richard Wright's startling and agonizing stories in *Uncle Tom's Children* display similar dispositions and strategies in the American South during the first few decades of the twentieth century. Countless other social memoirs and commentaries also engage those who desire to probe into the human condition.

SORTING THROUGH PUBLIC ISSUES

Many of life's moral norms are simple and clear-cut: Love is good; people deserve respect regardless of their looks; we should not harm others gratuitously. Often it is evident how to apply these norms in our individual lives. Public life, however, is more complex, and it is less evident how to apply moral norms to it. We do not always know what norms should be applied, especially when they conflict, and sometimes we do not know exactly what certain norms mean in a public setting. Those who like to think and probe take this complexity, conflict, and lack of clarity as an invitation to sort through the issues. Christians who do this are especially interested in how the issues connect with Christian values.

Consider, for example, the concept of justice. The first thought that comes to the mind of most people when they think of justice is due punishment for wrongdoing. This is natural, for the justice system is in the business of determining proper punishments for those who have broken laws. But there is another concept of justice. When Amos declares, "Let justice roll down like waters, and righteousness like an everflowing stream" (Amos 5:24), he does not have the due punishment concept of justice in mind. He does not refer to such a concept in the verses prior to or subsequent to his declaration. He does mention, however, treating the poor equally and fairly, not taking from them what rightly belongs to them. The justice he is expressing in this verse is tied to the idea of fairness and equal treatment of those at the bottom of society. And Amos is not the only one who employs this idea; other biblical writers do so as well. Consequently, it ought to be valued. This much seems fairly clear.

What is not clear is whether this second concept of justice should be valued more or less than the first concept, or more or less than other values, such as freedom. Nor is it clear what social patterns best exemplify it or what social programs best advance it. Should we make equal treatment of the poor a priority even if it means giving up some measure of freedom? Is due punishment so important that we should focus all our energy on it, even if that means we cannot expend energy on equal treatment of the poor? And what exactly does it mean to say that the poor should receive equal treatment? Does it mean giving up the principle that people deserve only what they merit? Should the wealthy be made to give up a certain percentage of what they have earned? These questions, which do not have easy answers, intrigue the active thinker.

DISCOVERING MEANING

One significant motive for thinking and reading is to discover meaning. I use "meaning" here in a broad sense. We want to know our place in the universe, in history, and in society. We want to discover values by which we can judge the importance of what we do. We desire to know what the cosmic significance of our life is. And although Christians have a sense of this significance, they want to know how everything else is connected to it. This broad sense of meaning has several components.

Finding Something Worth Living For

We are not satisfied with just knowing facts and getting information. Though finding bugs under a rock or stars in a galaxy delights us, we would feel incomplete if that is all we ever did. This sense of incompleteness does not disappear when we go beyond particular facts to general patterns, or when we find explanations for facts and patterns. Even putting our knowledge into a coherent system is not enough. We also want to know what makes our lives worthwhile, what is important and what is not.

This desire to know about our life's worth is more like a craving or driving force than an everyday desire. We can give up everyday desires fairly easily compared to surrendering this craving. It is not stretching things to say that we would sense a debilitating emptiness if we could not satisfy it. This is because we want our lives to count for something. We possess an intense need to make a difference, to feel in our hearts that what we do impacts others in meaningful ways.

Intellectual explorers feel this need as much as everyone else. Their explorations move past knowledge of facts and patterns, past explanations and coherences, to worth. They look for new ways to satisfy their craving for significance. Self-understanding for them, though valuable in itself, is also valuable because it awakens and solidifies moral sensitivities. Christians who like to think and learn know with the apostle Paul that if they have knowledge but not love, they are nothing (1 Cor. 13:2). So they use the inquisitive energy that propels them to gain the one to secure the other.

Feeling Keenly the Magnificence and Tragedy in Life

Those who like to think and learn also use their inquisitive energy to acquire certain feelings. They recognize that reality is not dull and flat but brimming with beauty and goodness and laden with tragedy and evil. Nature, they know, is more than matter in motion, and people are more than interactions of cells.

Beauty and goodness cause awe and delight, perhaps even exhilaration. The complexities of the human brain—the synapses and dendrites, the firing of the neurons and the traveling of electrical impulses along neural pathways—rouse wonder mixed with astonishment. The workings of a halfway house incite admiration for the patience of the supervisors and respect for the moral efforts of the clients. The knowing innocence of Prince Mishkin in Dostoyevsky's *The Idiot,* which differs from the naive innocence of a child, induces a mixture of wondering esteem and high regard. Sometimes these reactions are similar to the astonished gasp that one's first glimpse of the Grand Canyon or Niagara Falls elicits. More often they are like the calm and quiet awe that the still and motionless surface of a pond prompts.

Tragedy and evil, on the other hand, cause sadness, sorrow, and grief. This is true whether the tragedies happen to others or to oneself. If the tragedies are of one's own making, they evoke remorse and repentance. Although it is not pleasant to have these feelings, the one who grasps the reality of tragedy and evil does not evade them. Christians, in particular, do not avoid them, for they connect with the creation-fall-redemption theme that is central to Christianity.

This theme contains a blending of magnificence and tragedy. God has made us wonderfully good; we have spoiled ourselves; God lovingly offers to restore us. Some accept this offer, and some do not. This grand scheme prompts Christians not only to conceive all of life and reality in its terms but to respond with appropriate feelings and emotions. Delight and sorrow, awe and sadness are fitting responses to life Christianly conceived.

Pascal vividly displayed these contrasting stances in his depiction of the duality of human nature. We are both "judges of all things" and "feeble earthworms," he declared, both a "repository of truth" and a "sink of doubt and error." Overall, we are the "glory and refuse of the universe."[4] Pascal reacted to these "contradictions," as he called them, with astonishment, wonder, and admiration, on the one hand, and dismay, bewilderment, and a bit of horror, on the other.

Sensing the Divine

Possessing a sense of the divine is also part of discovering meaning. We are not content merely with what is temporal and finite. Something in us wants permanency, and we crave to be in touch with the infinite.

Often, though, this craving gets blunted by the distractions of our everyday duties. Our responsibilities consume the largest part of our consciousness, and only in rare scattered moments do we feel the craving. Even then it is weak and fragile. It disappears with the thought of our next task, or with an idle daydream, or even with the buzz of an annoying fly. Studying, learning, and accumulating new experiences can also distract us from the craving. They are, in fact, effective in that regard, for they keep our minds constantly occupied.

Even so, studying, learning, and accumulating experiences can awaken a sense of the divine in us. If stars "are telling the glory of God" (Ps. 19:1), then we should be able to see that glory in them. And if the virtues of one who has been awakened to things divine are "fruits of the Spirit" (Gal. 5:22–23), we should be able to sense God's handiwork in that person. Of course, it is not studying and learning alone that bring about a sense of the divine. It is our stance toward them that makes the difference—our active disposition to apprehend the divine through what we encounter.

GOOD OR BAD MOTIVES

Overall, then, people who like to think and learn are often driven by the five motives just described: a desire to know the way things are, a desire for coherence in their beliefs, a desire for self-knowledge, a desire to clarify public issues, and a desire to discover meaning, the latter of which includes three elements—a desire to find something worth living for, a desire to feel keenly the magnificence and tragedy in life, and a desire to sense the divine.

It may be, of course, that those who like to think and learn have other motives as well. In fact, it is likely that they do. Some may want to uphold a family tradition, find a cure for a rare disease from which a friend died, or defend their faith against attacks from nonbelievers. Some may have had a childhood teacher who stimulated their curiosity about a subject, and they are still impelled by that curiosity.

Other motives are not as respectable. Some may spend time thinking and learning for the public esteem it brings or to prove to themselves they are intelligent. For some the life of the mind is a way of becoming immortal through success and reputation. Still others have adversarial motives—a "desire to be in a position to force one's opinions upon others," a "desire to belong to a like-minded group of people who flatter one another by making fun of people whose opinions differ from those of the group," or a "desire to be one of a small group of enlightened ones who bravely struggle against the superstitions of the masses."[5]

It is even possible that some people who think and learn have no apparent motives at all. They simply fall into the life of the mind. It is something to do. Their friends are doing it, and they follow along, in the same way one cheers with the crowd at a baseball game—instinctively and unthinkingly.

Motives are complex, and we cannot always isolate them. But the five described in this chapter often operate in people, even if others also exist. These motives are valuable in two ways: They are good in themselves, and they bring about good. In other words, thinking and learning are intrinsically good and also good because of their effects. Chapter 2 deals with the first of these, and chapter 3 addresses the second.

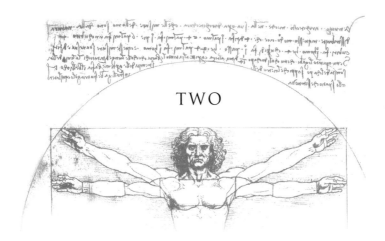

TWO

IS THINKING GOOD
FOR ITS OWN SAKE?

AMERICAN CULTURE is largely utilitarian. Indeed, nearly every culture is. This is because we humans are practical creatures—we like to get things done, and we like to figure out how to do them easily and efficiently. This is especially true in regard to our basic needs. "What first of all claims the attention of all creatures is the need to survive and, this being once reasonably assured, the need to exist as securely as possible," observes a contemporary philosopher. "All thought begins there, and most of it ends there. We are most at home when thinking of *how* to do this or that."[1]

It is not a bad thing to be practical or concerned with the hows of life. Most of what we do during the course of a day is aimed at getting things done—washing dishes, driving to work, cleaning the house, buying clothes. A large part of our thought life is practical as well. The mind is a navigator that gets us through the maze of a day's activities. It is an inventor that is constantly devising new ways of doing things. That is why our thinking is most at home with the hows of life, such as engineering, politics, and business.

If, however, the only matters with which we were concerned were the hows of life, we would be much impoverished. We would have no concept of why we act as we do, beyond, that is, immediate results. We would have no long-range goals and no sense that anything is good apart from its consequences.

Moreover, we would have no way of justifying why we should do anything at all. If we were to justify our actions solely on the basis of their consequences, and those consequences on the basis of their consequences, and so on, we would never reach a place where we could say, "This is good, just because it is." And without this stopping place, we would have no final basis for judging the worth of what we do.

Sadly, too much of life is barren in these ways. We accomplish things but do not ask why. Or we focus so much on results and consequences that we miss what is good for its own sake. We often treat thinking and learning the same way. We go to college so that we can have an assured place in the larger culture of which we are a part. We take courses so that we can enhance our résumés and get better jobs. We study computer science, chemistry, and biology to improve the technology of communication, transportation, and medical practice.

As worthy as these goals are, they are not enough. Life is more than results, and learning is more than studying hows. The "something more" involves intrinsic good. What is good about life itself, and thinking and learning in particular, comes from what is intrinsically good. This assertion does not mean that thinking and learning are not also good because of what we can do with them. They are. But they are also good "just because"; that is, they would be good even if they were not used for anything.

This thesis is not widely disseminated by educators, partly because they normally go about their jobs without explaining why they are doing so, but largely because such an idea is not prevalent among them. The American educational system has adopted the utilitarian disposition of the culture in which it is embedded. The point of an education, the culture declares, is to better oneself by gaining skills and knowledge that will be useful in the marketplace.

Rarely is the idea of learning as a good in itself mentioned. So while my thesis is not new, it is at variance with much of current culture, including Christian culture. Therefore, I have to develop the thesis. To do so I will explore the concept of intrinsic good, employ a couple of thought experiments to make the thesis convincing, and last, connect it to the notion of living more largely.

INTRINSIC GOOD

To say that something is intrinsically good means that nothing else is needed to justify it or make it good. It is an end-of-the-line good. We do not have to supply a reason for its goodness, as we would if we were sweeping the kitchen floor or doing the laundry.

By contrast, something that is good in a utilitarian sense is good because it brings about some other good. It is a means-good. If someone were to ask why we wanted something or were doing something, we would tell that person about the effect we hoped for. The goodness of the effect confers goodness on the act—the end justifies the means. Of course, if the means is counter to something else we hold dear, we would not regard the means as good. But if the means does not violate any moral principle, we say that it is good because of its good effects.

Examples of Intrinsic Good

To understand better the difference between these two kinds of goods, let's examine several examples that do not involve the life of the mind. The first example involves praise of God. "Praise the LORD!" David declares in Psalm 111. "Great are the works of the LORD, studied by all who delight in them" (Ps. 111:1–2). Suppose we ask, "Why should we praise God?" If we answer that we should praise God so that God will regard us favorably or so that we can have the peace of mind that comes from an other-directed activity, we are giving a utilitarian answer. But if we answer that we should praise God simply because it is proper to do so, we are saying that praise is intrinsically good.

This latter approach seems to be the stance the psalmist takes at least some of the time: "How good it is to sing praises to our

29

God; for he is gracious, and a song of praise is fitting" (Ps. 147:1). In this verse, praise is a fitting response to God's graciousness. Nothing is said about getting anything from the praise; its fittingness is sufficient for the praise. It is intrinsically good to delight in God's character and in what God does.

A similar point can be made about the admiration of beauty. Imagine that a traveler in the Wyoming Rockies encounters a magnificent display of snow-capped peaks. She might say to herself, "Ah! A good scene for a postcard," then take out her camera and get the scene on film. This would be an act of using the beauty of the mountains for a definite practical purpose. If, however, she were simply to say, "Ahhh," as an expression of her delight in the beauty around her, her stance toward it would not be utilitarian. She would be valuing the beauty of the mountains for its own sake.

Here is one last example. In his book *Pollution and the Death of Man: The Christian View of Ecology,* Francis Schaeffer distinguishes two stances we can take toward nature. One is utilitarian, and the other is respect based on nature's goodness. The first is the approach often adopted by environmentalists: We should treat nature well because we do not want to harm either ourselves or those who will live after us. Without disparaging this first stance, Schaeffer states that the second approach is the one that most truly derives from a Christian view of nature. According to this Christian view, Schaeffer argues, nature is good because God made it good. When we despoil nature, we are tarnishing something good, which means that the harm we do to nature is bad in itself. That is, it is bad apart from any harm we may cause to ourselves or others. And our respect for nature is good in itself—good independently of any consequences. It just is good.[2]

In each of the examples just given, the act is also good because of what it does. Praise of God calms us. Delight in an instance of beauty arouses sensitivity to human goodness. Respect for the value of nature incites a sense of divine goodness. And engaging in any one of these acts helps us chip away at the tight grip that our egos have on us. It is, in fact, characteristic of an intrinsic good that it has good effects. It would be odd if it did not. Although an activity that is intrinsically good would be worth pursuing even if it did not cause good effects, it is good for its effects too.

Intrinsic Good in the Life of the Mind

To say that thinking and learning are intrinsically good, then, is to say that they are good in the same way that praising God, admiring beauty, and respecting the value of nature are good. Consider some of the aims and ends described in the last chapter. Delighting in knowing the way things are is like delighting in the beauty of a landscape—we do it for its own sake, without thought of what we will get from it. Each kind of delight is a fitting and proper response, in the same way that praise is a fitting response to God's goodness. Landscapes are there to be valued for their beauty; bugs and stars are there to be known.

It is the same for sensing the divine. When we have a sense of the divine, we have no further end in view; it is valuable "just because." A sense of the divine, like praise, is an apt and rightful response to the presence of the divine. Feeling keenly both the tragedy and magnificence in life are also appropriate reactions, even though they may lead to nothing else. The sadness provoked by tragedy and the exhilaration occasioned by magnificence are emotions worth having regardless of any effects they may have.

Consider also the act of making beliefs coherent. We want to root out inconsistency among our beliefs and fit them together into a coherent pattern simply because doing so is good. This is especially so when we attempt to harmonize our Christian beliefs with our other beliefs. When we succeed in some measure, we can properly take delight.

Contrasts

These examples of intrinsic good associated with the life of the mind contrast with the idea that education is valuable because of what we can do with it. At a recent commencement of a Midwestern state university, the chancellor declared to the graduates, "Your accomplishments here will lead to important achievements on the road ahead." In a symposium on the future of Christian higher education, one of the authors asserted, "The purpose of Christian institutions is to educate students so they will be prepared for the vocation to which God has called them, enabled and equipped with the competencies necessary to think Christianly and to perform skillfully in the world."[3] Another author in the same symposium stated,

"Your college education provides the context for you to develop the disciplines of mind and life that will make a difference in your tomorrow."[4]

Chapel speakers at Christian colleges also refer to the idea that education is valuable for its usefulness. The Christian church, they say, needs leaders who will be effective witnesses to the Christian faith. College is a time of preparation for a lifetime of competent ministry, whether in the church or in the world.

It would be a mistake to say that the proponents of these ideas do not also believe that education has intrinsic value, for they no doubt do. It would also be a mistake to denigrate these ideas because they involve utility and not intrinsic value, for they affirm worthy uses of Christian education that are necessary in a culture that has lost its moorings. Still, the ideas contain the notion of an education's usefulness.

There is a distinct difference between these ideas and the ideas John Henry Newman employs in his classic book, *The Idea of a University*. "Knowledge is a state or condition of mind," Newman writes, "and since cultivation of mind is surely worth seeking for its own sake, we are thus brought once more to the conclusion . . . that there is a knowledge, which is desirable, though nothing come of it."[5] The phrase "though nothing come of it" expresses the key thought here. The reward of knowledge is not what comes from it; rather, it is its own reward. Simply having knowledge is rewarding; its worth does not derive from what we use it for.

To drive home his idea of knowledge, Newman compares it, as I have done, to beauty. But he goes one step further and states that the mind itself possesses beauty. It is not just that the intrinsic goodness of knowledge is like the intrinsic goodness of beauty, but that knowledge itself is beautiful. "There is a physical beauty and a moral; . . . and in like manner there is a beauty, there is a perfection, of the intellect."[6] In coming to have knowledge, we are doing what artists and poets do: creating beauty. "The artist puts before him beauty of feature and form; the poet, beauty of mind; the preacher, the beauty of grace: then intellect too, I repeat, has its beauty."[7] Beauty, of course, is intrinsically good, whether it be the beauty of a landscape, the beauty of a virtuous person, or the beauty of a cultivated mind.

The thesis that thinking and learning are good apart from their consequences should now be clear. Education, whether Christian or not, that aims solely at equipping students for work, ministry, and social change, though vitally significant, neglects an essential ingredient in a life well lived: the intrinsic goodness of knowledge. We certainly may value knowledge and the other aims of thinking and learning for their usefulness, but we should also value them without regard to their usefulness.

A DEFENSE OF INTRINSIC GOOD

What I have said so far has not been an attempt to support my thesis but merely to explain what it is. Of course, a fuller understanding of an assertion may convince someone of its truth. This may be the case here. The reader may be thinking, "Yes, I see what you are saying, and I see that it is true." Even so, I am not absolved from trying to show that it is true. This is what we turn to now.

Unfortunately, claims about intrinsic value are notoriously difficult to prove. The best one can do, it often seems, is simply to say, "I see intuitively that love, beauty, and knowledge are intrinsically good." Someone else could say, "I do not see that at all" or, "I see that they are good, but only because of what they do for us." What, then, can be said in favor of the claim that thinking and learning are good as ends and not simply as means?

The following two considerations are attempts to support this claim. Each consideration involves a thought experiment—imagining a condition that does not exist and asking what it would be like to experience that condition.

The Adam and Eve Experiment

Let us imagine what Adam and Eve might have done in their pre-fall state if it had lasted a century. By their pre-fall state I mean the condition they were in before they ate the fruit of the tree of knowledge of good and evil, before they resisted and hid from God, the time when they loved only goodness. Genesis 1 and 2 do not tell us how long this time before sin lasted. One gets the impression that it was not a very long period of time. Let us suppose, though, that it was.

Adam and Eve no doubt would have raised a large family and cultivated the land, as God had instructed them to do (Gen. 1:28). They would also have looked for fruit-bearing trees, delighting both in the fruit and the beauty of the trees (Gen. 2:9). Perhaps they would have taken some of their children along on their expeditions around Eden. They certainly would have been kept fairly busy during the first twenty or thirty years taking care of the growing number of young ones. But after their children had scattered, they would have had a fair amount of free time. What might they have done with it? Can we imagine them going on intellectual explorations—investigating the forests and fields around them and performing an occasional experiment?

They might have catalogued the various kinds of trees, animals, grasses, and birds. Perhaps they would have watched the flight patterns of the birds and made a scrapbook of the leaves of the various flowers they discovered. Maybe they would have blocked part of a stream to see how much faster water flowed when it went through a narrower opening. They may even have turned their gaze inward and observed their feelings and emotions. Perhaps they would have noted the degrees of delight they experienced and demarcated keen pleasure from calm contentment, and both of these from serious earnestness. In investigating their inner states, though, they would not have aimed at psychological health, inner balance, or freedom from compulsions, since they already enjoyed these.

We can also picture Adam and Eve linking all that they discovered to one central thought: This is what God has made, and it is good. They would have sensed the divine in what they learned and felt the splendor of God's works. And they would have wanted to expand the conditions in which they could encounter goodness and splendor.

Why can we imagine Adam and Eve doing these things? What is it about Adam and Eve that makes this scenario imaginable? The answer is that God put in them a desire to maximize goodness, because he made them like him. This means they instinctively would have wanted a life rich in goodness. Just as instinctively they would have known that one way to bring about riches of goodness is to obtain knowledge of good things. They would have delighted in this knowledge solely because they delighted in goodness and not because of any utility the knowledge had.

If we think that this scenario is possible, it is because we are assuming that knowing is good for its own sake. What the scenario illustrates is the following three-step argument:

1. What God has made is good.
2. It is intrinsically good to know what is itself good.
3. Consequently, it is intrinsically good to know what God has made.

When we take pleasure in knowing what God has made, we respond to it in the same way Adam and Eve responded in our hypothetical situation. We take the same stance toward it that God took: "God saw everything that he had made, and indeed, it was very good" (Gen. 1:31).

The Animal Experiment

Now imagine a situation that is even more fanciful than the one just described. Suppose that animals can explore and investigate. As things stand, of course, animals do not go around investigating to obtain knowledge. They "investigate" to find food, to keep themselves safe from predators, or to find an undisturbed site in which to nest. The "knowledge" they obtain, if that is what we can call it, is used solely to keep themselves alive. This, at any rate, is what we commonly assume about animals. If in fact they possessed knowledge for its own sake, not only would we be much surprised, but it would turn out that they are more humanlike than we suppose. To make this second thought experiment more graphic, picture a common backyard animal, a squirrel, going on knowledge expeditions.

After burying and retrieving seeds, this squirrel climbs down the tree in which it has been resting and makes its way toward a flower patch in a corner of the yard it has not visited recently. There it eyes a purple cone flower. The flower is too tall for the squirrel to inspect the petals up close, and its stem is too thin and unsteady for the squirrel to climb. So the squirrel reaches part way up the stem and pulls the flower over. The squirrel's front paws work their way along the stem until they reach the petals. When they get there, the squirrel bends the stem around so that it can see the petals from the top. It gazes at them for a bit, sniffs them, and lets the flower go. The stem straightens up. Then the squirrel goes to another flower and repeats this procedure.

The next day our curious squirrel decides to compare the shapes of the leaves on nearby trees. It snips a leaf from its own tree with its teeth, carries the leaf to the ground, and lays it at the base of the tree. Then the squirrel climbs another tree, snips a leaf from it, goes back down, and places it carefully beside the first leaf. After lining up half a dozen leaves, the squirrel sits in front of them. It rearranges the leaves once or twice, and after it has inspected them again, takes them to a low-lying bush, where it stores them.

What would we think if we discovered that squirrels could actually do these things? If we could get beyond the jolt to our image of subhuman creatures, we would recognize, I believe, that what they were doing has worth. Naturally, we might at first wonder what the point of their strange activity is. But that is only because we have become used to thinking of everything they do as entirely utilitarian. Once we saw that their investigations had no point beyond acquiring pure knowledge, we would realize that what they were doing had intrinsic value. If this is our reaction, it means that we recognize that human knowledge for its own sake also has intrinsic value. There is no difference, in theory at least, between a squirrel laying out leaves and a physicist working out the mathematics of subatomic particles.

These two thought experiments make evident the claim that "useless" knowledge has value. Its value is intrinsic precisely because it has no use. The first experiment also shows how possessing this kind of knowledge is a way of loving God.

LOVING GOD WITH OUR MINDS

Perhaps the reader has been wondering, "What does the fact that some knowledge is intrinsically good have to do with God? The greatest commandment is that we are to love God with all our heart, soul, and mind (Matt. 22:37). How does going after useless knowledge connect with loving or glorifying God?"

We have been working toward these questions, for the overall aim of this book, after all, is to explain the value that thinking and learning have for Christians. The answer: Possessing intrinsically valuable knowledge is a way of loving God.

C. S. Lewis maintained that the pursuit of intrinsically valuable knowledge can honor God. The pursuit he had in mind, he says, is "the pursuit of knowledge and beauty, in a sense, for their own sake, but in a sense which does not exclude their being for God's sake."[8] John Henry Newman, quoted earlier regarding his support of the idea that knowledge is good in itself, was also a Christian, and, like Lewis, saw such knowledge in a divine context. We can see what Lewis and Newman had in mind by looking again at the Adam and Eve experiment.

When Adam and Eve went looking for new kinds of flowers, they were exhibiting their love for God's good works. Their enjoyment in making discoveries about these works showed that their hearts were oriented toward God. All of their desires and emotions reflected that orientation, which is why they took keen pleasure in finding new ways in which God displayed himself. This certainly would count as loving God. Their knowing was both good in itself, because it was not used for anything, and an instance of loving God.

The kind of love involved might be called an intellectual love of God, or more simply, loving God with our minds. To love God with our minds does not mean that it is our minds that actually do the loving. Rather, we love God by using our minds. The situation is analogous to a surgeon who loves God with her hands— she uses her hands to express her love for God. Her hands are not doing the loving; she is doing the loving by using her hands. Both the surgeon and the learner can love God with all their hearts, that is, from the center of their personalities and with fervor and warmth. They do so through the special talents they have. Loving God with our minds, therefore, is no different from loving God with our hearts, or simply loving God. It is just a special way of doing so.

Two Qualifications

The alert reader no doubt has additional questions. "When you say that knowing the way things are is intrinsically good, do you mean that all knowing is good? And do you mean to imply that everyone should engage in the life of the mind?"

Does All Knowing Have Equal Value?

It certainly does not seem that all knowing has equal value or even that all knowing has value. Suppose someone embarked on a study of the number of oak trees in the town in which he or she lives. Knowing that number might have some use in assessing the ecological balance there, or it might become part of a larger picture in some way. But by itself, such knowledge seems trivial. Or suppose someone wanted to know about the secret sexual fantasies of an acquaintance. This knowledge might be useful in understanding the acquaintance, but by itself it seems perverse. For two reasons, then—triviality and perversity—not all knowledge has value. There is, in fact, a great deal that falls into these two categories.

This fact, however, does not invalidate the general thesis that knowing is good. The situation is like many others. Reading, for instance, is good. But some reading is trivial and some is harmful. The same is true of traveling, talking, listening, and other common activities. It also holds for research projects in the sciences and the humanities.

What knowledge, then, is intrinsically valuable? Unfortunately, it is not always easy to tell. Should we say that knowing the number of oak trees in a given town is trivial but that knowing the number of planets in our solar system is not? Should we say that wanting to know the sexual fantasies of our acquaintances is perverse but that wanting to know their ordinary dreams is not? It is not easy to draw a line between these cases. But, again, the case is similar to many others. We are not always able to draw a line between worthwhile reading and trivial reading. Yet we continue to think that there is a definite difference between the two. And we continue to come to new insights about what belongs in each category. We may, in fact, say that one of the aims of education is to discern what is worth knowing and what is not.

I want to propose one way of distinguishing the valuable from the trivial and the more valuable from the less valuable. John Henry Newman made this way a notable part of his concept of education. It is not just information we should be after, he says. Mere acquisition of isolated facts is not the aim of thinking and learning. The aim is, rather, to come to know the way facts fit together. What we need is "a connected view of old and new, past and present, far and near, without which there is no whole, and no center."[9] Our minds are not enlarged with the accumulation of more and more bits of data. "That only is the true enlargement of mind which is the power of viewing many things at once as one whole."[10]

For the Christian, the supreme connections among truths involve the basic tenets of Christianity. With these basic truths one can view "many things at once as one whole." There are, of course, lesser wholes, those involving connections within a particular science, for example, or those involving connections between different kinds of everyday experiences. These lesser wholes have value too, but their highest value comes from being linked to the ultimate truths about life and reality.

The first aim of thinking and learning described in the last chapter—knowing the way things are—needs to be modified, therefore. Some knowing is intrinsically good. And some intrinsically good knowing has more value than other such knowing. The second aim—making beliefs coherent—articulates an important way in which knowing comes to have more value. Christians in particular pursue this second aim, because they want to make sense of what they know by connecting it to their Christian beliefs.

Must Everyone Engage in the Life of the Mind?

The answer to this question is no. It does not follow that everyone should pursue the life of the mind because it contains intrinsic good, any more than it follows that everyone should take up drawing because producing works of beauty is intrinsically good. Other considerations are clearly involved, such as talent and social need. However, though the life of the mind is not for everyone, elements of it are vital to a complete and well-developed life. Consider an analogy using physical exercise. Even though exercise is good, it does not follow that everyone should be an athlete or participate in a sport. Still, it is good for everyone who can to engage in some physical exercise. Similarly, because the life of the mind involves intrinsic good, it enriches all those who engage in it to any degree. This becomes clear in light of the idea of living more largely.

LIVING MORE LARGELY

There are three ways of going wrong in life. In the first way, we do not act rightly. We break a law or act contrary to what God expects. The focus in this first way is on what we do. In the second way, the focus is on having the right desires and motives. We go wrong when we are consumed by envy or when we love with an ulterior motive. Each of these first two ways involves going against a norm. In the third way, we do not go against a norm but fail to have as many goods in our lives as we could. We live in a constricted way. The model here is Jesus' declaration in John 10:10: "I came that they may have life, and have it abundantly."

When we live in a constricted way, we close down. We do not look for opportunities to experience goodness. We restrict ourselves to narrow confines, as if we are holding up our hands, palms outward, and saying, "Stay away from me. I have my life set already." We miss the wideness that comes to those who are open to new possibilities. We do not take in the richness that presents itself to us. Living a constricted life is like reading second-rate novels instead of the classics, or eating macaroni and cheese out of a box every night. We get along, to be sure, but without the depth and grace of a master writer and without the pleasing tastes and nutrition of a variety of quality foods. It is not that we have done something wrong but that we are content with lesser goods.

When we live more largely, we actively look for fresh ways to experience goodness. We seek out new situations and activities. We are eager to embrace a wide array of good, as if we are holding our hands out in front of us, palms up and open, saying, "Come to me." Our basic orientation is different—we value the good we encounter and passionately want to increase it.

The contrast between these two kinds of living is illustrated in the comment that dying people sometimes make: "If I had the chance to live over, I would take more time to experience simple pleasures—the flowers beside the road, a walk with a friend, the little delights that come along every day." Those who say this regret that they limited themselves to a narrow range of experiences. They sense that their lives would have been richer if they had been more expansive.

The connection between living more largely and intrinsic goodness is simple yet potent: A larger life has more intrinsic good in it. Our squirrel, for example, expanded its way of being by pursuing knowledge for its own sake. We would not say, of course, that anything was amiss with its narrower way of being, because that is the way squirrels are designed to be. We, however, are designed to experience intrinsic good. When we do, therefore, we have more overall value in our lives.

This truth is displayed in the three intrinsically good activities described earlier: praising God, admiring beauty, and respecting the value of nature. If we engage in any one of these, we possess more richness than if we did not. And if we engage in all three, we possess still more richness. The same is true of the fruits of the Spirit listed in Galatians 5:22–23: love, joy, peace, patience, kindness, generosity, faithfulness, gentleness, and self-control. Having a few of these virtues is good, but having more is even better. If we possess them all, we possess an extravagance of goodness.

Therefore, if thinking and learning are intrinsically good, and if living largely involves maximizing intrinsic good, then thinking and learning contribute to a larger life. If we do not engage in these, we are not doing anything wrong. But we are missing out on something that would enrich us. We are missing the awe that accompanies knowledge of nature's intricacies. We are lacking awareness of our own deeper self. We are not experiencing pathos for tragedy or exhilaration for magnificence. We are failing to know the connections among the many facets of reality. We are possessing fewer ways of sensing the divine.

Perhaps one way to think of Christian redemption is that it saves us not just from the first and second ways of going wrong in life but from the third as well. Conceived in this way, redemption in Christ is aimed at restoring us to the pre-fall state in which Adam and Eve were naturally attracted only to goodness. It is designed to revive our lost proclivity to seek and exemplify a multitude of goods—moral, spiritual, natural, emotional, and intellectual. Under such redemption, we embark on a "pilgrimage of seeking to be fully alive."[11]

If what was said in this chapter is correct, attending school is not just a means of preparing for a good life. It is a good life. It is not simply a stage that gets us to the next stage. It is an end in itself. Studying and learning enlarge our lives independently of what they enable us to do later on. When we realize these truths, when we regard intellectual activities in their light, when we take to heart the fact that the intrinsic good associated with the mind raises the level of our existence, thinking and learning take on new life.

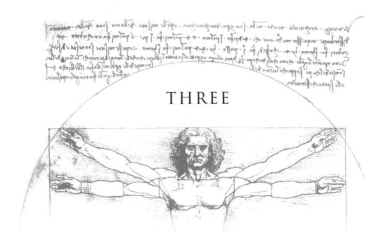

THREE

THE EFFECTS OF THINKING

FOR MORE THAN TWO DECADES of college teaching, I listed three objectives in the syllabi for the philosophy courses I taught: to become acquainted with core philosophical issues, to interact with these issues, and to assess them from a Christian perspective. These objectives varied a bit depending on the particular course I was teaching, but I never listed more than these three. It did not occur to me that the courses could have many more aims. And I never asked myself what else I wanted students to gain from a course. Courses were academic enterprises, I presumed, and should not be tainted with extraneous intentions. To do so would be to compromise academic integrity.

Then I changed. It wasn't just that my beliefs about courses changed. I changed. I began reading the novels of Fyodor Dostoyevsky and Leo Tolstoy. Some of their probing inquisitiveness into

43

human motivation rubbed off. I read some of the master analysts of the human condition—Augustine, Blaise Pascal, Ernest Becker, Søren Kierkegaard. I began listening to students in my office, at lunch, in the hallway, on the telephone. I discovered that they had deep feelings and dreams for the future. Then I turned forty and realized I would die someday. I asked students, "What do you like most about living?" I gradually became less of an emotional hermit and ceased regarding myself largely as an academic machine.

It occurred to me at some point during this transition that students are not just academic machines either. They participate in courses with a variety of emotions. They have memories of childhood experiences and past academic life. They want to be recognized by their teachers even if they do not get As. They struggle to become independent yet stay connected to home. They possess convictions about what is important. Most of all, they want to make a life for themselves. If they are persons of faith, they want to explore it or at least keep it intact.

Then one afternoon during the summer after my twenty-eighth year of teaching, a question hit me: What do I really want students to get out of my courses? I promptly got out a piece of paper and started writing. The list of objectives grew to thirteen. I wanted students to become more imaginative, more adventuresome, and more courageous. I wanted them to develop a passion for learning while maintaining habits of self-discipline. I wanted them to think for themselves and make the Christian faith their own. I also wanted them to become more prepared to die.

I put all these objectives on the syllabi for the next semester, varying them a little for each course. When I read the list during the first class period of Introduction to Philosophy (which I did with some trepidation), a few of the students snickered and several others smiled when I read, "to prepare you for dying." One of them asked about that one. I responded by saying I wasn't sure how it would work and that maybe it would have to be one of the course's mysteries. My sense was that the other objectives I added were a bit foreign to them as well. I reread the list during the last period of the semester and told the class I would be wildly delighted if they had attained just one or two of the objectives that semester. They didn't snicker this time.

This chapter addresses the effects of thinking and learning. I will not belabor the obvious: Through thinking and learning we gain skills that are useful both for particular vocations and for working in general, and we are enabled to live with an adequate degree of economic security. I will focus, rather, on several whole-life effects: the promotion of human flourishing, support of faith, and training in goodness.

PROMOTION OF HUMAN FLOURISHING

Two recent writers explain the biblical picture of human flourishing. "There is in the Bible a vision of what it is that God wants for his human creatures. . . . It is a vision of *shalom*," states Nicholas Wolterstorff.[1] Shalom means peace, but, he says, the biblical concept of peace includes more than what we might think of when we think of peace. It "incorporates right, harmonious relationships to *God* and delight in his service." It also "incorporates right, harmonious relationships to other *human beings* and delight in human community." Its last element is "right, harmonious relationships to *nature* and delight in our physical surroundings."[2] In shalom, we are not only in accord with God, other people, and nature, but we enjoy living with them, and even with ourselves.[3] Shalom possesses both a negative feature—the absence of hostility—and a positive feature—gladness.

Cornelius Plantinga also explains this concept of shalom: "In the Bible, shalom means *universal flourishing, wholeness, and delight.*"[4] In a world of shalom there would be

> strong marriages and secure children. Nations and races . . . would treasure differences in other nations and races as attractive, important, complementary. . . . Tow truck drivers and erring motorists would be serene on inner-city streets. . . . Intercontinental ballistic missile silos would be converted into training tanks for scuba divers. . . . People would stimulate and encourage one another's virtues. . . . Above all, . . . God would preside in the unspeakable beauty for which human beings long.[5]

In these manifestations of shalom, there is harmony among individuals and nations. People go out of their way to promote good. Respect, cooperation, helpfulness, and a sense of the divine predominate.

How do thinking and learning connect with this comprehensive vision of life? One significant way in which they connect is that we need impartiality and imaginativeness, two characteristics of good thinking, to discover this biblical vision. We need these two intellectual virtues so that our concept of biblical values is not bent by our own psychological traits or distorted by the specific faith tradition or culture of which we are a part. Let us focus on this last point for a bit.

Each of us grows up in a particular subculture—a subdivision of the larger culture—with its own distinct patterns and ways of thinking. To ensure that the subculture of which we are a part does not unduly shape our concept of biblical values, we may need to encounter other subcultures, for we do not always notice the values and patterns of the tradition in which we are immersed. By encountering other traditions, we will be able to disengage ourselves from our own. This will give greater scope to our moral perceptions. We will be able to let the Bible speak to us more directly and thus more accurately.

Picture a suburbanite who passes governmental high-rise residences each day as she drives to and from work—"the projects," which most suburbanites are fearful of encountering. The subculture of the suburbs comprises relative control and comfort, whereas the subculture of governmental high-rise living encompasses unemployment and constant struggle. If the driver never gets off the expressway, drives to the project buildings, and mingles with their residents, she will not be likely to know much about high-rise living (unless she studies it via articles and books). But if she immerses herself in the high-rise culture, her experience there will almost certainly enlarge her beliefs about the way things are and might broaden her vision of how things could be. She will be able to critique the subculture she regularly inhabits. If she is a Christian, she might discover truths enunciated in the Bible that she has missed, or she might change her view about which biblical values should have priority. With some imagination, she will be able to conceive of new ways of reacting to the high-rise subculture and to her own subculture.

The interaction between these two subcultures can work the other way as well. The high-rise residents can, theoretically at least, explore the life of the driver and have their concept of a just and equitable society enlarged. Both the residents and the suburbanite can convey truths to the other that the other may not have noticed. And together they can work toward making shalom a reality.

The interactions between these two subcultures are one form of the "praxis-oriented scholarship" that Nicholas Wolterstorff calls for. Praxis-oriented scholarship, Wolterstorff states, "analyzes social structures with an eye to the call for 'justice.'"[6] Doing this requires the ability to describe impartially both the social structures we inhabit and those that are foreign to us. Our aims include both the theoretical one of critiquing these social structures in light of the biblical vision of what God desires for us, and the practical one of enunciating particular means by which this vision can become a reality.

We can call praxis-oriented scholarship prophetic, in imitation of the Old Testament prophets, who applied God's commands to specific practices of the Israelites. The prophetic scholar does what Amos did when he declared, "Alas for those who lie on beds of ivory, and lounge on their couches, . . . but are not grieved over the ruin of Joseph!" (Amos 6:4, 6). Both ancient prophets and prophetic scholars join insights about divine truths with insights about actual practices to disclose a truth that was not evident before, or at least not evident to the untrained or spiritually myopic mind.

Prophetic scholars can focus on a number of subjects. They can study family life with a view to maintaining family stability. They can set up think tanks to work on scenarios for racial equity and international peace. They can work in laboratories to find ways to control industrial pollution and population-decimating plagues. They can study inner-city gang life, homelessness, and the circumstances of unwed mothers to set up effective programs that prevent such things. They can investigate the forbidden topics of suicide and incest among Christians to discover models of psychological and sexual well-being. They might even look into road rage and the driving habits of different segments of society to promote driving serenity. All of these areas involve dealing with the wounds of humanity.

Christian faith calls for three reactions to these wounds. It calls, first, for feeling them—for feeling the frustration of those who cannot easily extricate themselves from hopeless situations, for identifying with victims of parental betrayal or systematic oppression, for experiencing the pain of depressed adolescents. Christian faith also calls for thinking clearly and accurately about these wounds—for analyzing their nature, discovering their context, and uncovering their causes. Lastly, Christian faith calls for action—for founding and working with organizations that work with the wounded, for individual acts of compassion and justice, for political action. Those who engage in the life of the mind focus on the second of these. If they have balance in their lives, they will also take part in the first and perhaps some of the third.

If we lived as did Adam and Eve in a pre-fall state, we would not need to think about the wounds of humanity, because there would be none. Shalom would come to us naturally. As things stand, we need to work at shalom. The life of the mind is a part of that work.

SUPPORT OF FAITH

Faith, too, would come naturally if we lived in a pre-fall state. We would not wrestle with doubt and uncertainty about God. We would know instinctively that we were made by a divine being who intended for us to maximize goodness. This knowledge would not flicker but would constantly be with us, and it would direct our every move. We would not resist it or wonder whether it was right.

Tragically, we must continually shore up a faltering faith. On occasion, doubt comes to us unbidden; God feels absent; the thought that perhaps Christianity is all wrong springs to mind.

Before looking at several ways in which thinking and learning can contribute to a steady and sure faith, we need to deal with the objection that thinking has nothing to do with faith. It is an act of the will, not thought, on which faith depends, so this objection runs. It was an act of will that was the essence of Adam and Eve's fall—prideful rebellion. It is an act of will that is at the crux of the return to faith and at the core of making faith stable and strong—the softening of our resistance to God.

I think this view of the origin of sin is correct. At rock bottom our sinful nature is the result of an inexplicable turn away from God. If we try to explain this turning away by saying that we are not content with being creatures of God (or that Adam and Eve were not content with this), we have to ask why we are not content. Is this due to pride? Why do we have pride? Because we want to be better than God? Why? Sooner or later we have to stop and simply say, "We just resist God."

This fact, however, does not mean that thinking plays no part in our return to faith or in strengthening our faith. Thinking can be one of the factors that softens resistance to God. This is because willing does not exist in isolation. Willing and thinking interact in a variety of ways, many of them unnoticed by us. We do not just say, "I am not going to resist God anymore," and then not resist. The softening of our resistance comes bit by bit, with thinking, feeling, acting, reading, listening, and social interaction all included in the process. On occasion, the process speeds up and one undergoes a conversion or rejuvenation. But in this experience as well, willing, thinking, and feeling work together. We are not simply bare wills, pure thinkers, or sheer feelers.

Following are three ways in which thinking can support faith.

Finding Reasons for Believing

A couple of years after I graduated from college, I heard an Easter sermon in which the minister provided evidence for the resurrection, then responded to the swoon theory, the fabrication theory, the delusion theory, and other arguments resurrection detractors have used. It was not a passionate sermon. There were no ringing declarations of faith, just calm reasoning. I imagine some listeners were bored. Yet the sermon had a marked effect on me. I came away with a certainty that I did not have when the day began. Perhaps I had been in one of my doubting moods. Perhaps the fact that the sermon was a concise review of what I had encountered in a college class brought about the change. Whatever it was, it was a striking case of how reasons for faith can affect one's faith.

This same effect can occur when the comprehensiveness and the coherence of Christianity are spelled out. By comprehensiveness I mean the ability of an idea or theory to make sense of an extensive array of facts and experiences. If a theory is able to do this, we are justified in having more confidence in it. This is also true of coherence. If a group of ideas can be unified, that is, connected to several core ideas, we more readily assent to the ideas than we would if the ideas were disconnected and unrelated to each other. Together these two features of Christianity make it more convincing.

In order to see how Christianity is comprehensive, consider a few phenomena it explains. It explains reports of the resurrection of the unusual man from Nazareth by saying that he was divine. It accounts for the existence of a physical universe by appealing to the activity of an infinite, eternal, and all-knowing God. It states that humans experience guilt because they know they have violated the requirements of this same God. It explains both our proclivity for good and our penchant for evil by saying that we were created by God with this proclivity but that we tainted it by resisting goodness. It accounts for conversions by appealing to illumination and a change of heart on the part of the one converted, and to divine working on the part of God. Altogether these explanations contribute to what is sometimes called a "cumulative case for Christianity." With interlocking explanations, connected by the central Christian truths—creation, fall, and redemption—Christianity becomes more believable than if it had explained only a few isolated phenomena.

The comprehensiveness and coherence of Christianity can serve not only as support for a sagging faith but also as an intellectual witness to non-Christians. It is a common assumption of secular thinking that religious truths are in a compartment all their own. Belief in God is thought to have little to do with everyday life or with science, literature, or psychology. Christians, however, think of their Christian beliefs as being connected to everything they do and think, at least in their best moments. To show how this is the case is to show that Christianity is more credible than secularists suppose. It is to give "an accounting for the hope that is in [us]" (1 Peter 3:15).

Discovering the Need for Faith

In finding reasons for believing, we are doing something "evidential." That is, we are discovering why we should believe Christianity is true. In ascertaining the need for faith, however, we are trying to show that faith satisfies basic human needs. If we are talking to an unbeliever and explaining how Christianity meets basic needs, our enterprise would be "existential apologetics." Although it would differ from evidential apologetics, it would shore up our faith just as much, though in a different way.

A number of authors are worth reading to discover the need for faith. I shall mention two. Blaise Pascal wrote *Pensées* partly to give reasons for believing that Christianity is true but also partly to show that a Christian's faith best meets basic needs. Consider one of them: the need to fill the "God-shaped vacuum" within. We have an infinite abyss in us, Pascal declares, and "this infinite abyss can be filled only with an infinite and immutable object; in other words by God himself."[7] We try in vain to fill this abyss with everything around us. But these efforts will not work, since God alone is our true good. Pascal states, "Nothing in nature has been found to take [God's] place: stars, sky, earth, elements, plants, cabbages, leeks, animals, insects, calves, serpents, fever, plague, war, famine, vice, adultery, incest."[8] To these we can add romance, social status, admiration from our peers, owning quality possessions, career advancement, and, especially by those in academia, studying and learning. We use all of these to try to fill the God-shaped abyss within. If we are alert, we will notice that we do. We will recognize that our vague yearnings for something more, something that we dimly hope will be a final satisfaction, are really covert reachings for God. We will perceive, with Pascal, that we can possess this final satisfaction only if our yearnings are completed in faith.

Ernest Becker's *Escape from Evil* and his magisterial *The Denial of Death* are also worth reading for an analysis of spiritual experiences. We have two fundamental fears, Becker says, a fear of death with insignificance and a fear of too much life. We fear the former because we dread that death will bring to nothing our efforts to be remembered as individuals whose lives counted for something. We fear the latter because we are afraid of sticking out too much, which we will do if, morally and spiritually, we live richly and expansively. We compensate for our fear of death with insignificance by pursuing countless immortality projects, activities that we vainly expect will defeat death and give us a worth that will be recognized by all. We compensate for our fear of too much life by living in meager and restricted ways. God's grace gets shoved to the rear by our immortality projects, and courage gets defeated by our shriveled-up existence. It is only faith in the transcendent, Becker states, that can dissolve these fears.

What Pascal, Becker, and other writers teach us is that Christianity deals with foundational needs. Sometimes this is not readily observable. If we were to investigate church life as an anthropologist or sociologist might, we would notice the ways in which people in the church interact with each other. We would discover what practices are acceptable and unacceptable, and we would uncover patterns that those in the church might not be aware of. But we would miss the deeper significance of the church—to provide an antidote to guilt and death, to fulfill our deepest longings, to impart inner peace and unity, to confer cosmic significance on us. These are what really matter to us, and these are what Christianity purports to give.

Uncovering False Faith

A third way in which thinking supports faith is that it can help us detect false faith and lead us to true faith. The idea of false faith is simple: We think we have faith but in fact we do not. We do not, that is, have the saving faith Christianity calls us to. We have something that looks like it and that we mistakenly think is saving faith.

One form false faith takes is "crowd faith." Someone who possesses crowd faith so identifies with the faith of others that he comes to believe he has it as well. In reality, it is not his faith but that of others. He thinks it is his, though, because he does not distinguish himself from the others. He has become a "crowd Christian."[9]

This phenomenon is not unique to Christian contexts. Any time a cohesive group with strong ideals exists, those in the group are tempted to submerge themselves in it. And wherever there are leaders and people with strong personalities, which is everywhere, those who admire them are tempted to think they have the qualities of those leaders. These processes take place fairly unconsciously, so that those who have lost their identities in the group or admired person are usually not aware that they have done so.

What we need to uncover false faith is honest self-reflection. We need honesty because we do not like to admit, even to ourselves, that we have been mistaken. With honesty we can confess that we have evaded taking responsibility for our faith and have hidden behind the faith of others. We need self-reflection to discover the subtle mechanisms that lead to crowd faith.

The thinking and learning involved in this self-reflection differ from the thinking and learning involved in finding reasons for believing. When looking for reasons for believing, we direct our attention outward to evidence. When attempting to uncover false faith, we turn our attention inward. We sort through emotions. We poke around in our inner lives. We probe the half-hidden parts of our minds that lie underneath surface thoughts and feelings.

Several years ago I ran into a former student who said, "I remember your class well. That was where I lost my faith." "Oh," I responded a bit tentatively. "I lost my childhood faith and got a faith of my own," she explained. "Ahh," I said, smiling.

What this student no doubt meant was that her childhood faith was someone else's, perhaps her parents' or her church's, and that she had replaced this secondhand faith with a firsthand one. The point to notice is that it was largely intellectual activity that prompted her to do so. Her self-reflection led her to wonder whether she owned the faith she professed. And her intellectual exploration helped her find reasons for committing herself to faith.

TRAINING IN GOODNESS

We are told in Proverbs that if parents train up their children in the right way, when the children are old they will not stray from it (Prov. 22:6). The principle behind this truth is that good character can be shaped by proper conditions, especially in the young.

This principle holds for young adults less than it does for young children but more than it does for middle-aged people. Those in their late teens and early twenties are still developing their values; the books they read, the ideas they encounter, the experiences they undergo contribute significantly to what they will become. At the same time, though, they are not simply passive creatures who take in everything that comes to them. They also choose what they will experience and how they will be affected by what they experience, as do older adults. The apostle Paul recognizes this second factor when he declares to Timothy, "Train yourself in godliness" (1 Tim. 4:7). Paul is saying that we can intentionally cultivate a virtuous character. This section describes a number of specific ways in which we can use thinking and learning to do just that.

Taming the Fat, Relentless Ego

Iris Murdoch once wrote that "in the moral life the enemy is the fat relentless ego."[10] What she meant, in less picturesque terms, is that self-absorption is the main obstacle to being virtuous and that it is not easily arrested because it is so consuming. Self-absorption taints our perception of goodness so that we do not recognize that kindness, gentleness, and empathy enrich our lives. It also diminishes our desire for goodness. We are less moved to be kind, gentle, and empathetic than we are to indulge our own concerns. If, then, virtues, including the fruits of the Spirit mentioned by Paul in Galatians 5:22–23, are to get a foothold in us, we must tame the wild, expansive ego.

Unfortunately, there is no guarantee that a particular activity will help us do this. We can come away from anything we do with the same fierce self-absorption we had when we began. Still, some activities can help us become less self-absorbed. Playing together does this. Those who play together must consider the expectations of the others if the activity is to turn out well. Encountering the suffering of another also helps us to be less self-absorbed. We recognize that someone else has intense feelings and may need help or attention.

A number of activities involved in thinking and learning can have the same effect. Think, first, of listening. When we listen, we set aside our own concerns for a time so that we can pay attention to the concerns of someone else. We try to understand those concerns, without letting our own interests intrude. We may, of course, offer our thoughts, but this is conversation, not listening. Real listening involves checking self-absorption and focusing on the other. Listening in an intellectual context is the same. When we read, study, or listen to a talk, our aim is genuinely to understand the other person's ideas. To do so, we must temporarily suspend our own ideas and attempt to see the other's perspective. If the ego intrudes, no real understanding takes place.

Think, next, of discussing and debating. These require a demanding observance of the Golden Rule: "In everything do to others as you would have them do to you" (Matt. 7:12). When we explain our ideas, whether in friendly discussion or highly charged debate, we want those with whom we are interacting to focus on our central points and not peripheral ones. If someone were to react only to a peripheral point, we would feel that our ideas had not been treated fairly. We also want our ideas to be taken seriously. If someone were to respond with a clearly inferior argument, one that was plainly not well thought out, we would feel slighted. When we respond to others' ideas, therefore, we should try to ferret out what is essential in them and respond with considered reasoning. The ego, in contrast, would just as soon go for cheap victories, trampling others' views with irrelevant and easily refuted arguments. But there are no cheap victories in intellectual interaction, for a cheap victory is no victory at all. In intellectual matters, the ego's impulse to ignore and trample is constrained by the Golden Rule.

Think, last, of looking for magnificence and tragedy. In order to respond with awe to physical magnificence, we must attend to the complexity, intricacy, and grandness of what we observe. If it is moral magnificence to which we are responding, the splendor of virtuous action or character, we must attend to the moral grandness that is present. And if it is tragedy we are confronting, we must focus on the distress involved. In each case, our attention is focused on something other than ourselves. Our egos must let go of some of their self-directed engrossment.

Shaping Priorities

One of the most excruciating sentiments is to feel, during the final seconds of life, that we have wasted it. If we could picture ourselves drowning, unable to breathe and unable to save ourselves, with our life flashing before us and wholesale regret for what we had left undone consuming us, we might acquire a sense of this agonizing sentiment. Less torturous but no less significant is the regret we might have at seventy-nine as we reflect quietly on our life. "If only I had not let myself be so consumed with getting ahead; if only I had loved more widely, let my acquaintances into my life more, played more with my children; then— yes, then—I would have felt a larger contentment over the years."

It is not likely that we will drown and see our entire life flash before our eyes. Nor is it likely that at seventy-nine we will reflect on our life priorities unless we have made it a habit to do so in the decades before. Without this habit, we will barrel along at seventy-nine, at eighty-nine even, as if life has no end, ever postponing the question of what matters most. Our death will come unexpectedly, as death usually does, and we will have escaped the agony of a near-death flashback, but only by numbing ourselves to life's significant values and priorities.

One way to engender the habit of reflecting on priorities derives from the second aim of thinking and learning described in chapter 1: making beliefs coherent. When focusing on this aim, we attempt to connect our beliefs to a small number of core beliefs. For Christians, this means finding a central focus both for our concept of reality and for our concept of how we should live. The fact that we are creatures of a cosmic, divine being falls under the first of these; the fact that this being has an overall design for us falls under the second. Connecting the two means keeping God's vision for our lives in the forefront of our minds. It means evaluating what we do and do not do in terms of that vision. And it means ranking possibilities: This is important, that is trivial; this I need more of, that I need less of. The result is what Arthur Holmes calls a "unifying, consuming devotion to what is supremely good."[11]

Another way to engender reflection on priorities is to develop the imaginativeness involved in thinking and learning. We can do this by asking how things can be different. Getting in the habit of asking this question, however, is not easy either to initiate or to maintain. The culture of which we are a part has expectations and values that become ingrained in us, usually unconsciously. This unsettling fact means that the values of the culture to which we belong seem natural to us. To ask whether they could be different is disturbing, perhaps even wrenching.

The truly disturbing fact, though, is that some of these cultural values are alien to values Christians cherish. Indifference to violence, for example, has more and more permeated American culture. Sexual permissiveness has as well, and so has a hedonist mentality, whose message is, "at all costs, gratify your desires and drink at the bubbly spring of pleasure."[12] Consumption—constant buying of material goods—is also pervasive. Because these values seep into us, our priorities take on the shape of the indifferent, the permissive, the pleasure seeking, and the amasser of possessions. When, however, we ask how our values might be different, we imaginatively disassociate from what has become entrenched in us. We see the disparity between these ingrained values and the values we hold as Christians. We may even be moved to remake our priorities.

Such remaking is difficult, though, especially when we are not surrounded by others of like mind. Like the ember that goes out because it was separated from the fire, those who want to reshape their priorities will lose that desire if they are not near others with a similar desire. In a college setting, this means that Christian professors and Christians in administration must live their values. If they do not, students are likely to leave college with alien cultural values even more entrenched in them. Outside of college, Christians who like to think and learn will do well to associate with other imaginative Christians who are concerned about protecting their values from cultural influence.

Acquiring Habits and Virtues

It is sometimes thought that the life of the mind is completely different from ordinary life. No doubt this is true in some respects, but it is also true that both the life of the mind and life in general require the same habits and virtues. The following list describes characteristics that we can acquire through thinking and learning and that can be applied to life beyond the life of the mind.

Adventurous. Adventurous people are not content to stay in one place. They like to explore and take risks, knowing that what they do might not turn out as they expect. Intellectual adventurers investigate issues not thought about before, at least not by them. They go into unknown territory, taking the risk that they may discover unsettling truths. For them knowledge is not just given to them but something they pursue.

Passionate. Those who think and learn believe in what they do. They possess a lively interest in their investigations and invest energy in finding out more about life and reality. They care about clarity, consistency, and meaning.

Imaginative. Imaginative people view accepted truths in fresh ways. They seek alternatives to them and imagine how reality could be different. They like to dream up new possibilities. Learning for them is not simply a matter of piling up facts and bits of information. It involves asking creative questions and looking at the familiar from different angles.

Alert. Learners notice things that escape the attention of others because they actively look for them—the unsuspected pattern that explains a known fact, the psychological traits behind everyday behavior. Their minds are on the lookout for details that make a difference. They watch for intriguing departures from the normal yet are awake to what is fascinating in the normal. They are observant and attentive.

Gracious. Those who think and learn treat people who disagree with them graciously. They do not put others down; rather, they listen carefully and take what they hear seriously. They do not ridicule those with whom they differ. They defend their own beliefs without animosity, ill feeling, or unwarranted aggressiveness. People who engage in the life of the mind have plenty of opportunities to work on graciousness, for nearly everything they explore is drenched in controversy or discussion. Even when they do not actually confront those with whom they differ, they can develop a gracious disposition toward them.

Humble. Learners do not disdain those who have less education, nor do they view the acquisition of knowledge as a competition with themselves as the proud winners. They view others as equals and recognize that numerous people possess more knowledge than they do. Therefore, they do not flaunt their knowledge and are willing to listen to others.

Wise. Becoming wise is more than just becoming knowledgeable. Wisdom involves obtaining insight and discernment. Wise people sense what is important and what is not. They make sound judgments and exhibit perceptiveness. People can gain wisdom by sifting through the writings of respected authors, listening actively whenever the opportunity arises, expanding their experiences, and sorting the valuable from the trivial and the essential from the nonessential.

Attuned to God. Christian learners keep God in the forefront of their minds. They relate God to whatever they study, either in general ways or in specific and complicated ways. The general question they constantly ask is, "How does God as creator and redeemer connect to this new piece of knowledge?" The specific questions they ask about the relationship of God to their topic of study are as technical and complex as the subject they are studying.

Aware of sin and guilt. Christian learners also remember the fallenness of humankind. When studying the human sciences or when reading literature, they use, when possible, the ideas of sin and guilt as interpretive categories. They do not regard people merely as amoral creatures who have no sense of right and wrong.

Their aim is partly to fill out the biblical view of human nature and partly to make sense of the wide range of human experience.

Appreciative of redemption. In studying human nature, Christian thinkers and learners probe the depth of human motivation. They discover ways in which resistance and indifference to goodness work their way into our lives. They uncover our driving passions. As a result, they obtain a heightened perception of the depth of redemption. They know the intricate byways in the human psyche that God's grace travels. They comprehend the deeper emotions with which God's love connects. They understand why people both flee from grace yet cling to it.

To these characteristics we can add persistent, thorough, open-minded, courageous, and patient. All of these habits and virtues are demanding, not in the sense of requiring hard work (though doing anything of worth requires much effort), but in the sense of being difficult to acquire and maintain. It is not our natural disposition to be selfless and humble, nor are we normally inclined to be attuned to God. Acquiring these habits and virtues requires a transformed character as well as a good deal of "practice," neither of which comes easy. Because the life of the mind provides opportunities for practicing these virtues, it can contribute significantly to the moral and spiritual character of everyday life.

Encountering Grace

The central Christian reality is grace. "For by grace you have been saved through faith" (Eph. 2:8). It is by God's grace that we are absolved of guilt for our resistance to goodness. The forgiveness we experience when we accept God's grace gives us new motivation. We now urgently desire to excise envy, indifference, lust, pride, greed, and anger (though we also still want to hang on to these). Grace brings about gratitude, openness, gentleness, and a willingness to give. In a life of grace, we are slowly remade.

Are there ways of encountering grace in the life of the mind? Yes, opportunities for such encounters occur constantly while thinking and learning, just as they do in everyday life. As poet Maura Eichner put it, "Everywhere grace awaits."[13]

Grace can be seen in numerous characters in works of fiction: in Nathaniel Hawthorne's Dimmesdale, who rejects it; in Graham

Greene's whiskey priest, who wrestles with it; and in Fyodor Dostoyevsky's Raskalnikov, who finally embraces it. It can be seen in confessions, such as that of Augustine. It is present in plays and musicals, though frequently it is conspicuously absent. If we want to probe its nature, we can read works on spirituality, including those of early Christian authors such as the desert fathers and mothers. If we want to explore ways in which it can permeate our personalities and social structures, we can study psychology and sociology. We can find it, too, in poetry and history.[14]

The effects of thinking and learning described in this chapter deal not so much with what thinking and learning can do *for* us as what they can do *to* us. Put differently, the overriding value of thinking and learning is not to get ahead but to become certain kinds of persons. We become persons of faith who want to promote human flourishing and who desire to mature in goodness.

The case for the value of the life of the mind is now complete. But those who accept its value are not free from difficulty. The next two chapters deal with tensions between the life of the mind and Christian faith, and between the life of the mind and the wider culture.

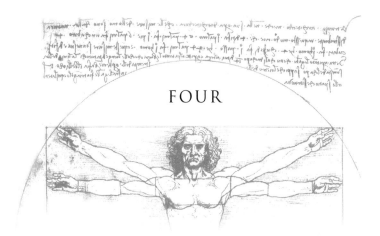

FOUR

TENSIONS BETWEEN THE LIFE OF THE MIND AND CHRISTIAN FAITH

IT IS TIME NOW to respond to the concerns raised in the preface. It is evident that not all Christians concur with those who are enthusiastic about thinking and learning. Some, in fact, have fairly negative sentiments about intellectual activities. For these Christians, thinking and learning are more enemies than friends, or their usefulness is limited to job training, promoting works of charity, or enhancing evangelism. The concerns of these Christians should be seen as rightful cautions but not fatal objections.

THE INCOMPATIBILITY OF FAITH AND INQUISITIVENESS

I have characterized thinkers and learners as inquisitive. Listen to someone who is suspicious of inquisitiveness: "Inquisitive people are always asking questions, always probing and poking around in new things. This means they are unsettled and never content. That might be okay for matters not involving faith, but for faith, it is lethal. People with faith possess an unshakable trust in Christ. They are content, settled, and secure, like a child who trusts her parents. Inquisitiveness, though, is consuming. Once you get it in your blood, it overpowers you, and you cannot get rid of it. You will wrestle with your faith until you die. What kind of faith is that?"

This objector points to a real tension between faith and inquisitiveness. Those who ask questions risk turning their faith into rootless exploration. And inquisitiveness can, indeed, be consuming; persons whom it has taken hold of almost certainly will wrestle with their faith.

The likelihood of tension, risk, and wrestling, however, is not a sufficient cause to refrain from engaging in the life of the mind. Such concerns certainly have not prevented people from embarking on marital relationships or deep friendships. Nor have they precluded the development of Christian communities or the endeavor to love. What the objector needs to show is that the risk involved in being inquisitive is too much for faith.

It has, indeed, been too much for the faith of some people. For them inquisitiveness has proved harmful and has undermined what they once thought was secure. They have asked and not found, or they have asked and found something different. But for many others inquisitiveness has supported faith by providing reasons for believing, by helping to discover the need for faith, and by uncovering false faith, as described in the previous chapter. Being inquisitive can also expand faith. When we are inquisitive, we explore new ways faith connects to life experiences. We ask how it can operate in work and play. We probe the nature of hope, forgiveness, and other key Christian concerns. In doing so, our faith opens up and spreads out. In addition, inquisitiveness can make faith more active and alive. Inquisitive people of faith look for fresh ways of living out their faith.

Moreover, being inquisitive does not just produce wrestling; it also helps Christians deal with times of struggle. Because faith does not come naturally, we will have to wrestle for it whether or not we are inquisitive. Children may spontaneously possess an unwavering trust, but the rest of us must wrestle with guilt, doubt, and deadly sins for this kind of trust. We can do so through prayer, silent meditation, active discussion with others, and also through inquisitive investigation.

The fact that inquisitiveness supports, expands, and enlivens faith and also aids in our wrestling with it counters the claim that being inquisitive presents too great a risk for faith. Though thinking, learning, and asking questions contain some risk, as does nearly anything worthwhile, the risk frequently does not have calamitous results.

Perhaps the objector will persist: "What you are saying sounds like spiritual schizophrenia. Having a settled faith and a restless curiosity is like sitting and walking—you cannot have both at once. A person who tries to have both will end up having neither or switching back and forth from one to the other."

It is true that a person of faith who is also inquisitive will find that her faith and inquisitiveness do not mix well at times. But it is also true that she can fuse the two so that they work together instead of pulling against each other. The best analogy here is not sitting and walking but being a pilgrim. Christian pilgrims have a solid faith yet are constantly searching. They are content in their faith, but at the same time they seek a higher spiritual level. They are learners who are happy with what they know but thirst for more. Though their faith is settled and secure, it is not stagnant. Their aim is to keep moving. Inquisitiveness, then, far from always constricting faith or sabotaging it, can be integral to it.

THE INCOMPATIBILITY OF FAITH AND IMAGINATIVENESS

Thinkers and learners are also imaginative. To this our objector may say, "Being imaginative is no more compatible with faith than is inquisitiveness. Those who are imaginative are constantly coming up with new ideas and creating new possibilities, which cannot be done to Christianity or personal faith. Christians believe in old truths, and our faith is not invented by us. We can, to be sure, grow in faith, but we do not look for a new faith nor do we imagine how our faith could be different. If we were to do so, we would distance ourselves from it. That would not be faith but a suspension of faith. Imaginativeness, creativity, and inventiveness are, like inquisitiveness, legitimate for matters not involving faith but not for faith itself."

The objector is right: Our stance toward faith cannot be one entirely of inventing and creating, or else our faith would dissolve. At the same time, it is just as injurious to exclude imaginativeness from faith, as will be shown. We need to find a middle ground in which imaginativeness nourishes faith without undermining it. This middle ground can be seen in the work of an artist.

Artists do not use pure imagination in drawing or painting. They have a goal in mind, and they know they must follow certain procedures if they are to achieve that goal. If they are Christians, they will want their art to display the divine in some way or at least be consistent with Christian values. Their finished work is a product of both structure and imagination, steady aims and inventiveness.

The Christian life can rightly be pictured as a work of art. It, too, is a result of structure and aim, on the one hand, and imaginative shaping, on the other. That is, the ideal Christian life displays both of these. Too often one predominates at the expense of the other, usually the former over the latter. When this is the case, structure and aim need to be balanced with originality and imaginativeness.

When we Christians exhibit imaginativeness in our thinking and learning, we are able to conceive of being "new creations" in Christ, with new desires and emotions. We can picture what it is like to be forgiven by God and free from guilt. Through the use of imagination we can devise fresh ways of being kind, gentle, and serene. We can escape the natural and secular in which we are so much enmeshed and break through to the supernatural. We can visualize a different future and engender hope for its realization. By listening to "the faint chattering of the songs that are to come," we can overcome despair, tragedy, and death.[1]

"No one who lacks imagination," Jill Baumgaertner declares, "can have faith."[2] Her assertion is not too strong. Without imagination, we would be stunted and constricted, unable to enlarge our faith. We would live so much by form and structure that we would risk turning our faith into what Graham ⟨…⟩e called the "habit of piety"—an empty faith, something th⟨…⟩ks like faith but in fact is not.³ Clearly, while the use of ima⟨…⟩n presents a danger to faith, a lack of imagination is just a ⟨…⟩erous.

The objector is right, too, to point out that wh⟨…⟩ utilize our imagination, we distance ourselves from faith. ⟨…⟩ we look at our faith imaginatively, we set it aside temporaril⟨…⟩ examine it in a detached way. Doing this too often may, inde⟨…⟩ninate the faith permanently. But it need not. Looking at o⟨…⟩ imaginatively is similar to an artist standing back a few st⟨…⟩urvey his work. Through such episodes of imaginative su⟨…⟩ʒ, we can observe the overall pattern of our faith, its high p⟨…⟩d its low points; we can notice features of it that normally es⟨…⟩ Because we are better acquainted with our faith, it can adva⟨…⟩mature.

"There is another angle to imaginativeness," a⟨…⟩e objector. "Christian community would be nearly imposʃ⟨…⟩veryone were constantly being imaginative. Community ⟨…⟩ adherence to standards and norms. With incessant creat⟨…⟩l inventiveness, the standards and norms of a group woul⟨…⟩down."

This is true. Imaginative people often do not fit ⟨…⟩n types of groups. Those who dream are sometimes seen as unacceptably different; they are blamed for threatening the established order and undermining group cohesiveness. Yes, it is difficult to maintain a stable and harmonious Christian community if it contains both those who conform to the accepted customs of the community and those who are highly imaginative.

The solution to this conflict between conformity and imaginativeness does not involve rejecting imaginativeness or throwing out all conformity. Rather, it involves working toward a balance of the two. Those who are imaginative need to feel accepted by their community, and the community needs to be assured of their loyalty. When the two groups learn to work together and discuss and explore traditions and new ideas in a constructive way, Christian thinking and learning can flourish.

THE POSSIBILITY OF ARROGANCE

We come now to a temptation to which those who think and learn are particularly subject. "Arrogance," states the objector, "is the inevitable sin of intellectuals. It comes in two forms: intellectual self-sufficiency and social superiority. Those who pursue matters of the mind are almost certain to have 'an unwarrantably high opinion of human natural powers,' their own included. They are prone to trust 'in their own wisdom rather than submitting the mind humbly to the truths of holy scripture.'[4]

"This is why Paul declared that 'knowledge puffs up' (1 Cor. 8:1). The acquisition of knowledge makes us think we can figure out life by ourselves. It causes us to rely on ourselves more than is justified, that is, in a cosmic, spiritual way that undermines childlike trust in God. We are tempted to think of ourselves as worthy of respect and esteem because of our knowledge. Piling up knowledge is a little like building a tower to God. The science that Western civilization has gorged itself on for the past two or three centuries is similar to the Tower of Babel—a monument to human godlikeness. Or so we suppose.

"There is more," says the objector. "Those who consider themselves intelligent and who read and study are likely to think of themselves as superior to those who are not intelligent and who do not read or study. In our culture, differences in social classes are determined largely by differences in intelligence and education. And belonging to a higher social class invariably tempts us to think that we are better than those who are lower on the social scale.

"The trouble with succumbing to these temptations," the objector concludes, "is that doing so imperils faith. Exaggerated self-reliance and social superiority conflict with the humble submission to God required by true faith. Why, then," asks the objector, "should we engage in intellectual activities when we know that our faith will be damaged?"

We must acknowledge these temptations. They are hazards distinct to those who pursue the life of the mind, even for short periods of time. Nathan Hatch, himself a Christian thinker, put it correctly: "The Christian scholar walks a precarious path because the deadliest vices of all, autonomy and pride, are so pervasive and so beguiling within academe."[5] However, these temptations are not reason enough to shun intellectual activities, for every activity and occupation has its special temptations. Social workers, for example, are liable to think they have control over their lives because they come into contact with so many who do not. Undertakers are tempted to become numb to the pain of death. Christian ministers may substitute sermons on compassion for real compassion. The life of the mind has no corner on temptations, and we may engage in it with the same vigilance with which we engage in other activities.

To avoid pride and autonomy, however, we must regard our intellectual capabilities rightly. Doing this involves keeping their importance in perspective. Those who spend time thinking and learning tend to magnify the significance of these activities and to judge nearly everything else by whether it fits into an intellectual mold. To avert this arrogant attitude, we need to remember that we are more than just minds. We are also bodies, emotions, and relationships. We are bundles of desires and centers of action. Recalling these obvious facts reminds us that we are the same as everyone else.

Keeping our intellectual capabilities in perspective also involves not using them to justify ourselves. I use "justify" here in the sense in which Jesus used it in the story of the Pharisee and the tax collector: to make ourselves right before God. The Pharisee conceived of himself as right in this way because he was not a thief or a rogue, as was the tax collector (Luke 18:9–14). Those of us who become absorbed in intellectual activities sometimes imagine that thinking and learning not only make us better than others but also good in God's sight, almost as if our standing with God were determined by them.

We can evade intellectual arrogance by keeping God's grace in mind. When we do, we will not use our intellectual capacities and accomplishments to justify ourselves. Grace is a leveler, and when we realize that it is by grace that all are saved, both intellectuals and nonintellectuals, we will consider ourselves equal to those who do not pursue the life of the mind.

Further, we can avoid arrogance by associating with people outside our usual circle. Perhaps we can spend time with those at the bottom of the economic ladder—those who are often seen as less educated and therefore less intellectual. If we resist the impulse to demonstrate our superiority and simply let ourselves enjoy their company, we will see them as fellow human beings who are equal to us. Perhaps we will even encounter someone who, despite not having a college degree or a high-paying job, has intellectual insights we may not have considered.

Finally, as mentioned before, we must always keep in mind that we have much to learn and that there will always be people who know more than we do and from whom we can gain new insights and knowledge.

THE NEGLECT OF EVANGELISM, COMPASSION, AND JUSTICE

The objector is not finished: "We are commanded to go into the world and make disciples (Matt. 28:19–20), which we cannot do if we devote time to intellectual activities. Nor can we attend to the poor, the sick, the homeless, the imprisoned, and those who are unjustly discriminated against if we are occupied with reading and studying. C. S. Lewis put it this way: 'He [the Christian] must ask himself how it is right, or even psychologically possible, for creatures who are every moment advancing either to heaven or hell to spend any fraction of the little time allowed them in this world on such comparative trivialities as literature or art, mathematics or biology.'"[6]

I have several responses to this concern. The first is that we can do evangelism and perform works of compassion and justice when we are not studying and learning. This, after all, is the way most people operate. They spend time in volunteer programs when they are not at their jobs or doing other good things. The objector is certainly correct to point out that those who are attracted to the life of the mind should not become so immersed in it that they neglect compassion, justice, and evangelism. Such a life would, indeed, be one-sided, but the same could be said of a life that focused completely on one thing of any sort. To be consumed by one kind of activity, no matter how good it is, is to live an impoverished life.

Second, we can fulfill the Great Commission and do works of compassion and justice through intellectual activities, not just in addition to them. We can use the content of what we study to make disciples and to show compassion. Being a disciple of Christ involves our minds as well as our hearts. Those who think and study can contribute to this mental aspect of discipleship by clarifying, explaining, and defending aspects of faith and justice.

Consider two examples. It is an established fact that African Americans have a much higher unemployment rate than most other segments of American society. If we could determine the causes of this phenomenon, we could construct workable remedies. It would be an exercise of compassion and justice to ferret out the causes and make them known. It is also an established fact that incest occurs in Christian families at roughly the same rate as it does in non-Christian families. Knowing what lies behind this phenomenon would help us to devise models of healthy Christian families. Again, an intellectual activity could promote compassion and justice.

Finally, in response to the objector, many significant biblical values exist. Making disciples of all nations is not the only activity in which Christians should engage. Other activities are not only biblically sanctioned but also required of us. We are to cultivate a wide array of virtues, such as those mentioned by Paul in Galatians 5:22–23. Cultivating these virtues makes us more Christlike, which certainly is an important aspect of the Christian life. Keeping ourselves free from idols is another biblical value, and worshiping God is still another. These might be categorized as "life enrichment aims." They surely are part of what Jesus meant when he declared in John 10:10 that he came to give us an abundant life.

If, then, the life of the mind contributes to life enrichment, we may legitimately engage in it. The objector's concern, therefore, does not undercut the value of the life of the mind. As Harold Heie put it, "Scholarship informed by Christian perspectives is kingdom work, just like evangelism is."[7]

THE INCOMPATIBILITY OF THOUGHT AND DEVOTION

The objector has a final concern: "Thinking may support devotion to Christ, but it is more likely that it will subvert devotion. The essential ingredient of Christian devotion is personal experience—the experience of God's forgiveness, adoration in worship, openness to grace, and the like. Thinking, however, objectifies our personal connection with God and makes it impersonal. If we are going to be serious about our faith, we should reject what undermines personal experience with God."

It is true that thinking at times objectifies devotion. On occasion it turns a personal faith into a mere cerebral one. When it does so, experiences with the living God are replaced with concepts.

Those who believe that faith involves passion often voice this suspicion regarding the life of the mind. Søren Kierkegaard, a nineteenth-century Danish philosopher, was one such person. For him, "faith is indeed the highest passion of subjectivity."[8] He contrasted this "passion of subjectivity" with understanding and objectivity, which involve pure thinking and passionless concepts. If all that we have is understanding and objectivity, Kierkegaard asserted, we are still pagan: "The one who has objective Christianity and nothing else is *eo ipso* a pagan, because Christianity is precisely a matter of spirit and of subjectivity and of inwardness."[9] Moreover, Kierkegaard stressed the power of objectivity to undermine subjectivity. "In this objectivity one loses that infinite, personal, impassioned interestedness, which is the condition of faith."[10] In other words, when we immerse ourselves in the pursuit to understand Christianity, we may forget that the point of Christianity is to be a Christian.

Surely Kierkegaard's observations are correct. Notice, though, that Kierkegaard is not saying that Christianity contains no objectivity. He is saying that with understanding only and no subjectivity ("objective Christianity and nothing else") we will not have faith. Kierkegaard himself advocated a good deal of thinking about faith via self-reflection. Here, then, is the key in responding to those who are suspicious of thinking: We need to combine thought and passion.

What would such a combination look like? It would be a thoughtful devotion, a clearheaded passion. Both thought and devotion would be in each other's service—thought clarifying and deepening devotion, and devotion keeping thought from becoming sterile. We can see how the fusion works by looking at two who exemplified it: Socrates and Jesus.

The central focus of Socrates' life was the pursuit of virtue. He cared more for the souls of his fellow Athenians than he did for wealth and fame. At the same time, he exhibited the highest intellectual standards, which he employed in his pursuit of virtue. He made significant distinctions and drew out the logical consequences of ideas. He zeroed in on central themes and elucidated his ideas with precision. He was, in sum, both passionate and thoughtful.

Jesus, too, fused these two characteristics. The Sermon on the Mount displays both moral urgency and the intellectual ability to state ideas simply and directly. His interactions with those who wanted to trap him exhibit a high degree of cleverness. His parables embody insight into human nature; his pronouncements are clear and precise; his debates with his detractors reveal surpassing acumen.

We do not ordinarily think about the intellectual characteristics of Jesus, partly because we focus on the content of what he said, but mostly because we look past his human features. When we notice them, however, we find a high level of thoughtfulness, intelligence, and discernment, each of which is fused with the moral and spiritual content of his message. If, then, we take Jesus as a model, we will want to maintain both our devotion and our thinking at the highest levels. It may not be easy to do this, but it will not be because thinking conflicts with devotion.

The objections to thinking and learning contain significant insights that Christians need to keep in mind. But they do not establish that the life of the mind invariably weakens Christian faith. Given the good found in the life of the mind, we may actively pursue it.

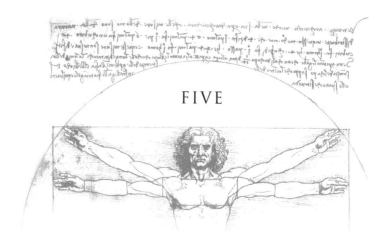

FIVE

IS THE LIFE OF THE MIND AT ODDS WITH CULTURE?

IF WE STRETCH our imaginations a bit, we can picture a culture that values the life of the mind. It would be a culture in which poets and astrophysicists were esteemed more than entertainers and sports heroes. Lectures on aboriginal Australian music or recent developments in Russian literature would evoke more interest than prime-time television programs. Participants in book discussion groups would outnumber spectators at sports events.

If picturing such a culture makes us smile, it is because it differs so much from the one in which we actually live. The one in which we live has features that do not fit well with the aims of thinking and learning described in chapter 1. These features are, in fact, in sharp tension with those aims. Some of the tensions make it more difficult for anyone to pursue the life of the mind, and others make it more difficult for Christians in particular to do so. This chapter describes both kinds of tensions, beginning with those of a broader nature and ending with those that affect Christians specifically. Through these descriptions, I hope to point out some prominent hazards to the life of the mind and also say more about what is involved in engaging in it.

THE VALUES OF POPULAR CULTURE

One hazard originates from the well-known phenomenon of group influence: We are shaped by the groups of which we are a part. We take on their values, adopt their unwritten assumptions, acquire their conceptual frameworks, participate in their rituals, and partake in their accepted behavior. There are, to be sure, people in every culture who do not fit in, who are part of a distinct subculture, or who disdain what they conceive to be popular. These people are not affected as much by the values of the wider culture. For most of us, though, it is an unquestioned fact that culture molds us.

The power of this molding has been noted by numerous observers of the human condition. Plato's vivid imagery in *The Republic* captures the point well. In the book Socrates declares that the public trains up "young and old, men and women alike, into the most accomplished specimens of the character it desires to produce." It does so

> whenever the populace crowds together at any public gathering, in the Assembly, the law-courts, the theater, or the camp, and sits there clamoring its approval or disapproval, both alike excessive, of whatever is being said or done; booing and clapping till the rocks ring and the whole place redoubles the noise of their applause and outcries. In such a scene what do you suppose will be a young man's state of mind? What sort of private instruction will have given him the strength to hold out against the force of such a torrent, or will save him from being swept away down the stream, until he accepts all their notions of right and wrong, does as they do, and comes to be just such a man as they are?[1]

We do not, of course, need public gatherings of the sort Socrates described in order for group influence to work. The mass media and public education work just as effectively. So do daily interactions with others, both inside and outside our immediate families. Plato's picture of group influence applies to actual crowds and to subtle social dynamics alike. Though the clapping and booing of others cannot be heard, they have the same outcome.

Following are three values in popular culture that are at odds with thinking and learning.

Getting Ahead

The populace clamors its approval of those who climb the ladder of social success. It cheers when people achieve a recognized status and claps when they become widely admired. If we let ourselves be affected by this cheering and clapping, the intrinsically valuable goods of thinking and learning will become less appealing to us, for by themselves they do not bring us social status or wide admiration. Society does not applaud when we make a new discovery about ourselves or apprehend the magnificence of a fictional character's conversion or the tragedy of oppressive social structures.

We can, of course, try to get ahead in one segment of our lives and value knowledge for its own sake in another. But a divided life is decidedly unsatisfactory. We will be pulled in different directions, without a center to which we can hold. If we are to love thinking and learning, we will have to tune out the cheering and clapping of the crowd.

Speed

Our culture also applauds speed. We like our computers to be fast, and we like to drive fast. We have little patience for extended analyses of social issues—anything more than two or three sentence encapsulations is nearly intolerable. Drawn-out scenes on television or in movies are also unendurable; we like short, quick takes that change rapidly.

If we assimilate this desire for speed, we will not be able to maintain the patience and persistence required for thinking and learning. To obtain self-knowledge or clarify public issues, we need prolonged attention. This involves steady efforts and periodic staring-out-the-window time, whether in libraries or in the comfort of our living room. When we possess this unhurried frame of mind, we will say with Aristotle, "One swallow does not make a spring, nor one day."[2] We will realize that just as we need a lifetime to work on virtues, which was Aristotle's point, so we need long years to pursue thinking projects.

Entertainment

We are a culture that cheers entertainment. We like to sit and gaze. We spend endless hours staring at moving images of people on a flat screen and at their real counterparts in public stadiums and auditoriums. All we have to do is take in what we observe. We do not need to interact with or respond imaginatively to it.

Thinking and learning, however, require a good deal of lively and energetic interaction with the object of our attention. To those who have become accustomed to being entertained, this interaction will feel strange and even alien. To pursue the life of the mind, they will have to set aside their impulse merely to gaze and adopt different inclinations.

THE REIGN OF TECHNOLOGY

The pervasiveness of technology in Western culture has become so commonplace that we scarcely notice it. But if people from the past were to visit, they would observe its mark both inside and outside our homes, in cities and on farms, in stores, in drawers, and on shelves. They would be amazed at what we regard as ordinary and mundane.

Suppose our visitors questioned our motives. "Why do you want so many machines, computers, implements, engines, and appliances?" they might ask. "They are everywhere!"

"For efficiency," we certainly would reply. "We can do more with less effort."

"Yes," our visitors would respond, "we can see that. At the same time, we also observe that you put a great deal of effort into being efficient. So simple efficiency does not explain what is really going on. What is behind your endless pursuit of efficiency?"

This question might leave us tongue-tied.

"Maybe you like the sense of power that technology gives," the visitors would continue. "Your extraordinary machines make you feel that you have a great deal of control."

If this suggestion is correct, we have the seeds of hostility between technology and the life of the mind. Power is beguiling. If we let it become our primary motivation, we will not take to thoughtful reflection very easily. We will like the feeling of energy spurting through our limbs more than the contemplation of virtue, and we will want to pursue control rather than sort through the tangle inside us. We will be more interested in saving time than in ferreting out magnificence and beauty.

Perhaps our visitors from the past would remark that we are obsessed with technology and power. If that is on target, then technological pride will move us, not care for our souls or love of the good. Such pride does little to nourish the pursuit of intrinsic good in the life of the mind. Obsession with technology combined with a materialist bent will cause us to use technology to pile up possessions and construct instruments of power. The larger aims of thinking and learning will be lost.

While our visitors from the past have insightful observations, they are overlooking another feature of technology. It accomplishes an enormous amount of good. Largely due to it, for example, the life expectancy in the United States increased from 47 to 76 during the last century. Moreover, it employs the very traits required for thinking and learning: reflection, imaginativeness, and inquisitiveness. To say that we cannot have both efficiency and thought is not true. Power and intellectual exploration can coexist.

Technology, therefore, is two-sided. It is consistent with thinking and learning; indeed, it springs from the desire to think and learn. But our passion for technology can crowd out the pursuit of knowledge for its own sake. We must try to keep what is good in technology without letting it corrupt our desire for a different kind of goodness.

THE MARGINALIZATION OF CHRISTIANITY

Our century is also one in which Christianity has taken not second place but third or fourth, especially in academia. Many colleges and universities that were founded by Christians have departed from their founders' aims, and nearly all the major universities in the United States are secular. Christianity is regarded by many professors as quaint, antiquated, or a threat to an open exploration of ideas—in any case, not worth serious consideration.

The Christian who ventures into academia will feel like Plato's young person who entered a hostile crowd. He will find it difficult to resist the crowd's pressure to join its clamoring. His friends from outside the crowd will fear that the crowd will be his undoing. And it might be. Even the Christian who pursues the life of the mind on his own might succumb to the pressure of the crowd. Many of the best books in numerous fields of study are written by non-Christians. Crowd pressure for the solitary thinker and learner comes not so much from secular academic institutions as from the content of what is studied and the general intellectual milieu in which he studies.

By entering the crowd, the Christian takes the risk that his faith will slip away. Both the direct and subtle coercion of the crowd may undermine what once was firm and secure. His desire to be part of the crowd may be so strong that he will do what he believes he has to in order to remain in it.

If he does keep his faith intact, he runs the risk that he will put it into a separate compartment reserved for his private life and his forays back to the life he shares with his Christian friends. When he is with them, he will display the marks of genuine faith, but when he is in the crowd, he will act as if his faith has no connection to what he studies.

He also runs the risk that the assumptions of the crowd will seep into his thinking unbeknownst to him. If this happens, he will take on the crowd's agenda and adopt its modes of thinking. Though he retains his faith, it will be tinged with alien motifs.

These possibilities have actually happened to numerous Christians who have entered academia or pursued the life of the mind. The crowd has been too much for them. Others, though, have not succumbed. They have been able to hang on to their faith and to work at integrating it into their crowd life, endeavoring to be part of the crowd while not being a crowd person. They have done this by associating with those in the crowd yet retaining their Christian values, by adopting some of the crowd's aims while rejecting others. They are like Christians who are in the world but not of it. This is not an easy trick to pull off, they know, but they are convinced that it is worthwhile.

THE POSTMODERN TURN

Thus far we have been examining tensions between Christian thinkers and secular culture. Now I want to backtrack a bit and say that using Plato's crowd image to depict the relationship between Christians and secular culture is a little misleading. That relationship is not entirely one of antagonism. Secular life is a web of complex strains, some of which conflict with Christianity and some of which do not. To sustain authentic Christian thinking, we need to sort through these strains, accepting them when possible but discarding them when not. It may be that segments of the crowd are not as antagonistic to Christian faith as we suppose. It could, of course, turn out that the crowd is even more antagonistic than we think.

One prominent movement we need to sort through is postmodernism. Those who participate in the life of the mind, whether in college or on their own, will not get far before encountering this movement. It has spread to large segments of academia and even to popular culture. In some places, it is orthodoxy—an unquestioned ideology that reigns supreme. Many Christians view postmodernism negatively. Our stance toward it, they say, should be to uphold Christian truth against it. Since academia has become infected with it, Plato's picture of a young person holding out against the crowd is, indeed, an apt metaphor of the Christian intellectual who is surrounded by postmodernists.

This view has a large measure of truth to it. Postmodernism may influence Christians in a negative way, causing them to let their faith slip, to compartmentalize it, or to let it be tinged with alien motifs. But it is also true, I believe, that postmodernism can have desirable effects on Christian thinking. Let us consider some key elements of postmodernism to see how they fare.

First, however, we need to recognize that postmodernism is a complex and varied phenomenon. Postmodernists focus on many different themes and even disagree at times. In order to get a handle on postmodernism, I will compare it to modernism, since postmodernists generally reject the main themes of what has been

78

called the modern age, which has existed for roughly the last four centuries. The modern age is not entirely over, though, despite claims that we live in a postmodern age. Modernism continues to exist in various parts of academia and American culture.

A first theme of modernism is that truth is objective; it exists independently of human perceptions and social circumstances. A second theme is that we can know these objective truths about reality, whether this reality be physical, social, human, or literary. A third theme goes a step further: We can have confidence in our ability to know ultimate reality; we do not need divine revelation to discover truths about God and our destiny. A fourth theme extends this confidence to our ability to know objective moral truths.

Postmodernists typically deny all or nearly all of these claims. Truth is not objective but relative, most postmodernists say. This means there are no universal truths, that is, no truths that everyone is obliged to believe, whether about reality, literary texts, or morality. Different beliefs arise out of different cultures, and conflicting cultural beliefs are equally valid. This cognitive and ethical relativism has undercut the modernists' belief that we can discover objective truths, because there are no such truths to be discovered. This is not traditional skepticism, we should note, since skeptics normally believe that truth, if we could know it, is objective. Nevertheless, it is a skepticism of sorts; modernists were wrong to have such an extreme trust in human abilities. Other postmodernists who do not adopt the relativism of these postmodernists still share their distrust of the ability to discover objective truth.

Clearly, the relativism in postmodernism conflicts with the traditional Christian belief that Christianity is objectively true. As a result, Christians who are surrounded by postmodernists may find themselves under severe attack. This is particularly true if postmodernists believe that Christians are arrogant in thinking that they know what is objectively true and intolerant of those who do not concur with them.

We ought not be too categorical in pointing out the antagonism between postmodernism and Christianity, however, for postmodernism contains lessons for Christians. One is that we need to be cautious about what we declare as absolute truth. Though theological truths such as Christ is divine and God is Triune are absolute, it does not follow that our favored form of worship ought to be universally embraced. We need to look carefully at our beliefs in light of postmodernism's insistence on the cultural origin of our beliefs. We may find that some of what we believe is derived more from our culture than we suppose.

Postmodernism also teaches us to tolerate diversity. Christians have not always done well in this regard. Western Christians have sometimes disparaged Russian spirituality or Latin American theology. White male theologians have had little use for African American or feminist theology, and vice versa. All Christians need to appreciate different Christian traditions without giving up belief in the objectivity of truth. They need to demonstrate that one can believe in objective truth without being arrogant toward or intolerant of those who differ from them.

It is pertinent to point out, as well, that modernism is no more congenial to Christian faith than is postmodernism. Though we can welcome modernism's belief in objective truth, we should be hesitant to endorse its claims regarding the sufficiency of human reason to know all the truth we need to know. An overconfidence in human abilities can undermine our reliance on God's revelation through Scripture and the awareness of our need for God. This, in fact, has happened during the course of modernism's development since the seventeenth century. The modern age has fallen prey to the temptation of intellectual arrogance more than seems likely with postmodernism.

This brief survey of cultural forces has shown that Christian thinkers are surrounded by a wide variety of voices. The right attitude to have in regard to these voices is to sort through them, value those that are true and right, lament those that are not, and dialogue with their proponents, if one can, with the aim of being a Christian voice among them.

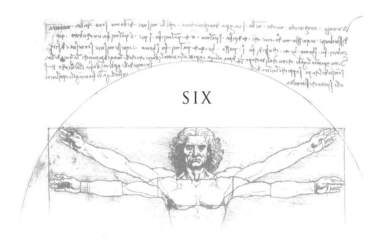

SIX

THE CROWD
AND THE COMMUNITY

THE PEOPLE IN PLATO'S CROWD hold undesirable values, and the young person in it is trying unsuccessfully to remain free of their influence. Now imagine a crowd different from the one Plato depicted. This crowd is made up of people of faith who love what is truly good and right. They do not blindly chase after power and possessions or pursue narrow and constricted goals. They are also learners who like to explore and create. They are gracious to one another, humble in their claims, and constantly on the alert for ways they can fuse their faith with their learning.

This new crowd is not wild and raucous, as was Pla but calm and friendly. Rather than cheering and cla unbridled frenzy, it gives encouraging smiles. Our yo does not need to be constantly on his guard against it. Instead, he feels supported by it.

We might call this faith and learning crowd a "community," for "crowd" has negative connotations, similar to those of Friedrich Nietzsche's derogatory term "herd," or Søren Kierkegaard's disparaging phrase "crowd Christians." Nietzsche, Kierkegaard, and Plato all distrusted the "masses," which they thought lead people astray more than they steer them right. Our remade community of learners, though, influences people in positive ways more than negative ways. Though we cannot give the community absolute trust, we do not need to be incessantly suspicious of it.

The faith and learning community's power to mold for the good is reason enough to become a part of it. Joining such a community is wiser than removing oneself entirely from Plato's boisterous crowd and becoming a loner. Most people who try to pursue a project on their own discover that it is difficult to keep going. What we do alone is likely to become a halfhearted effort or wither away. This is as true for the life of the mind as it is for maintaining an active Christian faith.

When we surround ourselves with others of like mind, we are stimulated to devote our best efforts to shared aims. We are moved to learn simply by being with others who do so. The model here is the formation of faith: "Faith and moral formation," Arthur Holmes observes, "are acquired usually and best, not by force of argument or weight of objective evidence, but by entering into the life of a community and making its heritage one's own."[1] When we embrace a Christian community of learning, our own Christian learning develops and matures.

The kinds of groups I have in mind are book discussion groups, study seminars, groups that meet for lectures and poetry readings, Sunday morning adult forums, and Christian colleges. Even an occasional conversation or a visit to a library or bookstore can act as a community of learning. All of these communities possess an atmosphere that tends to rub off on us when we are in their presence.

THE BENEFITS OF A COMMUNITY

What characteristics do such groups have? The most obvious one is that a lively interest in learning is prominent in them.

In a college, for example, teachers express their enthusiasm for thinking and learning, partly to engender student interest but mainly because it is one of their life passions. Students, too, are avid learners. Even though most of them will not end up pursuing the life of the mind full-time, many wholeheartedly adopt its aims while in college.

In addition, those in Christian communities of learning foster an ethos of distinctively Christian learning. They try to avoid a split between Christianity, on the one hand, and learning, on the other. In particular, they want to exemplify the virtues and habits that are characteristic of Christian learners. They are motivated to extend their Christian ideals to the intellectual realm. In a college, both teachers and students spend time in and out of class exploring ways in which their study areas connect with Christian truths. They regard their learning as a genuinely Christian activity, not just as an interesting hobby or passing interest with no cosmic significance. To them, intellectual exploration is part of a larger set of commitments that gives it meaning.

A further feature of communities of learning is that their leaders and teachers consider themselves learners. We must not assume that teachers have stopped learning just because they have an advanced degree and hold an official position. Learning for them is a lifelong process; they are still students in an important sense. This means that both teachers and students think of themselves as equals, without, however, subverting the teacher-student relationship.

Lastly, those in Christian communities of learning make special efforts to cooperate with others in the community. They do not compete with one another to see who can be the best or who can be the most prominent. This kind of competition often provokes alienation and turns learning into a rancorous game or an unbridled means of self-justification. Genuine learning communities encourage their members to work with each other instead of against each other.

COMMUNITY DANGERS

We should not suppose, though, that there are no dangers associated with a Christian learning community. Plato, Nietzsche, and Kierkegaard were correct to notice that groups cannot be invested with complete trust. Two perils come to mind. One is that a defensive mentality can overtake a Christian group. In other words, the group begins to see itself as an outpost of truth in a wilderness of rampant falsehood. The principal activity of such a group is to defend itself against attacks, and therefore, most of its energy goes into fighting secular culture. The trouble with this defensive mentality is that the love of knowledge for its own sake tends to get lost in the conflict with the enemy. It also obscures the enemies in our own hearts. A genuine community of learners, however, strives for balance. It responds to outsiders who differ from it, pursues the intrinsic goods that come with thinking and learning, and encourages its members to reflect on their own inner lives.

A second peril associated with a Christian community of learners is that it can squelch open inquiry. It does so by prizing conformity more than imaginativeness, by exerting pressure on its members to comply with its expectations more than allowing them to develop freely. Members of a group do, indeed, need to share some ideals, or else the group would not exist. What tends to happen, though, is that these ideals harden into unquestioned orthodoxies. Ways of acting, manners of speaking, and leading beliefs become fixed. These unwritten standards then turn into boundaries.

Some members of the group who are aware of the boundaries may feel hampered in their explorations. Others in the group will be unaware of these boundaries; their intellectual life will become uncritically narrow because it springs indiscriminately from the group. The ideal Christian community of learners again strives for balance. It esteems both imaginativeness and shared ideals. It also knows that the tension between the two is sometimes sharp, but it does not give up either because of this.[2]

Other perils exist as well. In any learning community, some members will rise to the top, and as a result, others will battle envy. Pursuing excellence will undermine some members' reliance on God's grace. Others will find their identity more in being an intellectual than in being a child of God. All will be tempted to become crowd Christians, that is, to let the Christian faith of the community become a substitute for their own faith.

The antidote for these perils and temptations is to become an "individual"—not a solitary individual but a community individual. An individual makes up her own mind and takes responsibility for her own beliefs. She does not identify with the community so undiscerningly that she loses her own identity. She is, in short, her own person. At the same time, she gladly contributes to the life of the community and allows the community to contribute to her life. She does not live for herself alone; her aims coalesce with those of the community. Though she is aware of her individuality, she is also attentive to her connection with others in the community.

Two examples of faith and learning communities, the first a poetry discussion group and the second a weekly roundtable discussion, show such communities in action. The poetry discussion group reads two or three poems at each meeting from the works of George Herbert, T. S. Eliot, Wendell Berry, Maura Eichner, and other Christian poets. The leader presents the ideas in the poems, explains obscure terms, unpacks special images, and raises questions. Members of the group add their thoughts throughout the session, and both the leader and the participants gain insights from the contributions of each other. Their openness to fresh perspectives evokes a higher degree of imaginativeness than they normally experience. Their commitment to Christian thinking acts less as a boundary than as a rich source of ideas.

The weekly roundtable discussion is held in the cafeteria of a Christian college. Its leader is a faculty member who poses a question for each week's discussion, and its participants are students. The leader acts as a moderator to keep the discussion moving; he asks questions and makes comments on points that are made, listening attentively to all that is said. Discussions are sometimes one-sided and occasionally get bogged down on side issues, but often they are creative explorations from which both the faculty member and the students profit.

Christians who like to think and learn thrive in groups such as these. We may not be able to avoid a Plato-type crowd, but that should not prevent us from drawing sustenance from an alternate community.

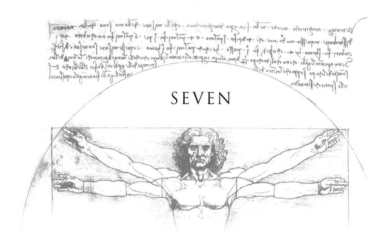

SEVEN

THE HERMIT
AND THE EXPLORER

PICTURE TWO PEOPLE, one a hermit and the other an explorer. The hermit shuts herself off from contacts with other people and also, let us suppose, from feeling and thinking. She displays few signs of vigor. When she ventures out for supplies, those who encounter her notice her reticence and indifference. She responds to queries with an ambiguous head movement, makes no eye contact, and initiates no conversations. In the privacy of her self-constructed cage, she sits and stares. Hardly anything interests her, and nothing moves her to action except necessities. When she does move, it is with sluggishness. She is a perfect specimen of the living dead.

The explorer, however, is open to what the hermit has closed off. She has an animated interest in the people she encounters and asks about their hopes and dreams. When she listens, her face lights up. She displays spontaneous delight when making new discoveries. She does not wait for adventure to happen to her; she seeks it out, sometimes with a bit of fear but always with anticipation. No cage can hold her. Perhaps she travels, but she does not need to go far, for she finds treasures everywhere. Her inner life is also rich; she has an extensive array of thoughts and feelings. If Socrates or Kierkegaard had encountered such a person in one of their daily excursions, they would have exclaimed, "Aha! Here is one who is fully alive!"

Real hermits, we should note, are often more like the explorer than the above depiction suggests. They may cut themselves off from others in order to probe their inner selves. Or they may do so to pray or pursue wisdom. This is especially true of the early desert Christians. After a dozen years alone, they returned to civilization transformed. That could not have happened if they had simply stared dully at the sand on which they sat.

Real explorers, too, often have some hermit in them. Though they are open and active in some respects, they may be minimally open in other respects. They may, for example, energetically explore the mountains of Colorado and Wyoming but be somewhat reclusive, or they may be exceptionally approachable but unresponsive to art and poetry.

The truth is that we are all partly explorer and partly hermit. We go after new experiences, but only in certain ways. City life may strike us as attractive, but love may seem fearful. Or we may like to dip into classic fiction but avoid sorting out our emotions.

One way to think of the larger life God desires for us is to see it as a way of minimizing the hermit and maximizing the explorer in us. God invites us to feel, love, act, and think. To do so, we cannot sit and stare. We must get up and look around. I do not mean that we must go places and take in new sights, for we can be explorers wherever we are. Those with whom we live and work possess depths that can be endlessly plumbed. Our backyards are unexplored wildernesses. Books contain inexhaustible riches, and so do our own inner selves. Explorers track down fresh life, love, and thought wherever they are.

Writer Wendell Berry vividly portrays the temper of the explorer. Mat, an eighty-year-old native Kentuckian, comes upon a stream in a forest behind one of the pastures on his farm. "A water thrush moves down along the rocks of the streambed ahead of him, teetering and singing. He stops and stands to watch while a large striped woodpecker works its way up the trunk of a big sycamore, putting its eye close to peer under the loose scales of the bark. And then the bird flies to its nesting hole in a hollow snag still nearer by to feed its young, paying Mat no mind. He has become still as a tree, and now a hawk suddenly stands on a limb close over his head. The hawk loosens his feathers and shrugs, looking around him with his fierce eyes. And it comes to Mat that once more, by stillness, he has passed across into the wild inward presence of the place.

"'Wonders,' he thinks. 'Little wonders of a great wonder.' He feels the sweetness of time. If a man eighty years old has not seen enough, then nobody will ever see enough. Such a little piece of the world as he has before him now would be worth a man's long life, watching and listening. And then he could go two hundred feet and live again another life, listening and watching."

Mat realizes that his unexpected experience is a little like God's constant experience. "For a second he feels and then loses some urging of the delight in a mind that could see and comprehend it all, all at once. 'I could stay here a long time,' he thinks. 'I could stay here a long time.'"[1]

A hermit would not be aware of her surroundings in the way Mat is. She would regard the stream simply as a means of marking her location. The water thrush and striped woodpecker would be nothing more to her than irrelevant objects. They certainly would not be worth watching or listening to. Mat, however, takes keen enjoyment in their movement. He could watch them for a considerable time without tiring, maybe even for a lifetime. He senses that his rapturous absorption mirrors God's, but he cannot hold that thought long lest his mind explode with the largeness of it.

Christian intellectual explorers are like Mat. They watch and listen and become intrigued by the events they encounter. They put themselves in positions in which they will make new discoveries. Because they are Christians, they regard their discoveries as "little wonders of a great wonder." They also conceive of their intellectual exploration as a response to a number of divine invitations.

One of these invitations is to acquire a diversity of goods associated with the mind. This invitation is based on the intrinsic goodness of the aims of intellectual exploration described earlier—the good of knowing God's creation, the good of thinking coherently, the good of sensing profoundly the magnificence and tragedy in life, the good of knowing one's own inner terrain. The richness in possessing these goods is like the profuseness of Mat's experience after he entered into "the wild inward presence" of the place by the stream.

Christian intellectual explorers also respond to the invitation to understand their faith. This invitation is based on the biblical portrayal of people as holistic—feeling and acting creatures who also think. This concept of human nature spurs explorers to elucidate the content of their faith and to reflect on its nature. It moves them to relate their faith to the various contexts they inhabit. Doing so is similar to Mat's act of connecting his experience of the little place he occupied to the "great wonder" of the universe.

Another invitation is to describe the results of one's explorations to those in secular culture. This invitation is based on the biblical admonition that Christians be witnesses to their faith. It involves understanding the mind-set of those in secular culture and stating Christian truths clearly and thoroughly. If Mat were to tell others of the wonders in the woods, he would be doing something akin to this.

God extends other invitations to us as well; some relate to intellectual exploration and some do not. God invites us to make music, listen to the lonely, and correspond with prisoners; to write stories, feed the homeless, and translate the Bible into new languages; to paint paintings, write poetry, and drill wells in primitive villages in impoverished countries.

We cannot, of course, respond to every invitation. Nor should we feel that we must do so. Interest, talent, and circumstance play important roles in determining our responses. Some people, for example, may engage in prison ministry full-time, some part-time for a limited period, and some not at all. It is the same with intellectual exploration. Some may engage in it as a full-time vocation, others as a part-time pursuit, and still others as an occasional activity.

We are called, however, and not just invited, to regard all these invitations as worthwhile—they come from One who values each of them. This means we should be glad whenever any one of them is pursued by someone, even though it is not one we ourselves have embraced. Intellectual explorers should encourage and admire those who listen to the lonely, and well drillers should have the same stance toward those who write or draw.

We are also called to accept one or more invitations. Too few Christians do that. The deadly sin of indifference keeps us sitting and gazing. The values of popular culture pull us away from God's values. And suspicion about some of the invitations prevents us from valuing them.

If what has been said in this book is correct, Christians should value intellectual exploration. With our talents and circumstances in mind, we should adopt the aims of the life of the mind and exemplify the habits and virtues of the Christian mind. When we do so, we will, like Mat, listen and watch, reveling in the wonder we encounter at the stream of life. And our lives will be immeasurably enriched.

APPENDIX

QUESTIONS
FOR REFLECTION

1. Is "tending the garden" (Genesis 1 and 2) as legitimate as fulfilling the Great Commission (Matt. 28:19–20)?
2. What does it mean to love God with our minds?
3. How can we deal with the tension between confident faith and searching inquisitiveness?
4. Are there limits to curiosity?
5. How would church life be different if there were more imaginativeness in it?
6. Are art and music intrinsically good?
7. Is the life of the mind an escape from real life?
8. Why do Christians sometimes feel threatened by those who ask questions?
9. Must all Christians be thinkers and learners in some way?
10. Is it possible to live a rich Christian life as a "simple soul," that is, without deep thinking?
11. What turns knowing into an idol? What is the difference between regarding knowledge as an intrinsic good and idolizing knowledge?

NOTES

CHAPTER 1 WHY DO WE LIKE TO THINK?

1. A. G. Sertillanges, *The Intellectual Life: Its Spirit, Conditions, Methods* (Cork, Ireland: The Mercier Press, 1948), 73.

2. Steven Weinberg, *The First Three Minutes: A Modern View of the Origin of the Universe,* updated ed. (New York: Basic Books, 1993), 102.

3. There are other considerations that add to the plausibility of the big bang theory than the two I have mentioned. See Weinberg, *The First Three Minutes;* and Martin Rees, *Before the Beginning: Our Universe and Others* (Reading, Mass.: Helix Books, 1997). Some Christians are as suspicious of the big bang theory as they are of the theory of evolution. The big bang theory, however, is governed by laws and observational discoveries in astronomy and astrophysics that have nothing to do with biology.

4. Blaise Pascal, *Pensées,* trans. A. J. Krailsheimer (Baltimore: Penguin Books, 1966), 64 (#131).

5. Peter Van Inwagen, *Metaphysics* (Boulder, Colo.: Westview Press, 1993), 16.

CHAPTER 2 IS THINKING GOOD FOR ITS OWN SAKE?

1. Richard Taylor, *Metaphysics,* 4th ed. (Englewood Cliffs, N.J.: Prentice-Hall, 1992), 1.

2. Francis Schaeffer, *Pollution and the Death of Man: The Christian View of Ecology* (Wheaton: Tyndale, 1970).

3. David S. Dockery, "The Great Commandment as a Paradigm for Christian Higher Education," in *The Future of Christian Higher Education,* ed. David S. Dockery and David P. Gushee (Nashville: Broadman and Holman, 1999), 9.

4. Bob R. Agee, "Values That Make a Difference," in *The Future of Christian Higher Education,* 201.

5. John Henry Newman, *The Idea of a University* (Notre Dame: University of Notre Dame Press, 1982), 86.

6. Ibid., 92.

7. Ibid.

8. C. S. Lewis, "Learning in War-Time," in *The Weight of Glory and Other Addresses* (Grand Rapids: Eerdmans, 1965), 49.

9. Newman, *The Idea of a University,* 101.

10. Ibid., 103.

11. Karen A. Longman, "Envisioning the Future of the Christian University," in *The Future of Christian Higher Education,* 43.

CHAPTER 3 THE EFFECTS OF THINKING

1. Nicholas Wolterstorff, "Teaching for Justice," in *Making Higher Education Christian: The History and Mission of Evangelical Colleges in America,* ed. Joel A. Carpenter and Kenneth W. Shipps (St. Paul: Christian University Press, 1987), 210.

2. Nicholas Wolterstorff, *Until Justice and Peace Embrace* (Grand Rapids: Eerdmans, 1983), 70.

3. Ibid.

4. Cornelius Plantinga Jr., *Not the Way It's Supposed to Be: A Breviary of Sin* (Grand Rapids: Eerdmans, 1995), 10.

5. Ibid., 11–12.

6. Wolterstorff, "Teaching for Justice," 213–14.

7. Blaise Pascal, *Pensées,* trans. A. J. Krailsheimer (Baltimore: Penguin Books, 1966), 75 (#148).

8. Ibid.

9. Søren Kierkegaard has a good deal to say about crowd faith. He attacked it vehemently in his *Attack upon "Christendom"* (trans. Walter Lowrie [Princeton: Princeton University Press, 1968]), and many of his other works contain subtle psychological analyses of it.

10. Iris Murdoch, "On 'God' and 'Good,'" in *Revisions: Changing Perspectives in Moral Philosophy,* ed. Stanley Hauerwas and Alasdair MacIntyre (Notre Dame: University of Notre Dame Press, 1983), 72.

11. Arthur Holmes, "Integrating Faith and Learning in a Christian Liberal Arts Institution," in *The Future of Christian Higher Education,* ed. David S. Dockery and David P. Gushee (Nashville: Broadman and Holman, 1999), 156.

12. Douglas Frank, "Consumerism and the Christian College: A Call to Life in an Age of Death," in *Making Higher Education Christian,* 259.

13. Maura Eichner, "Out of Cana," in *Unfolding Mystery: An Anthology of Contemporary Christian Poetry,* ed. David Impastato (New York: Oxford University Press, 1997), 163.

14. Nathaniel Hawthorne, *The Scarlet Letter;* Graham Greene, *The Power and the Glory;* Fyodor Dostoyevsky, *Crime and Punishment;* Augustine, *Confessions;* Benedicta Ward, trans., *The Sayings of the Desert Fathers.*

CHAPTER 4 TENSIONS BETWEEN THE LIFE OF THE MIND AND CHRISTIAN FAITH

1. From Wendell Berry's poem, "Manifesto: The Mad Farmer Liberation Front," in *Unfolding Mystery: An Anthology of Contemporary Christian Poetry,* ed. David Impastato (New York: Oxford University Press, 1997), 160.

2. Jill Baumgaertner, "Faith and Imagination," in *Should God Get Tenure? Essays on Religion and Higher Education,* ed. David W. Gill (Grand Rapids: Eerdmans, 1997), 162.

3. Graham Greene, *The Power and the Glory* (New York: Bantam Books, 1968), 161.

4. Nathan Hatch, "Evangelical Colleges and the Challenge of Christian Thinking," in *Making Higher Education Christian: The History and Mission of Evangelical Colleges in America,* ed. Joel A. Carpenter and Kenneth W. Shipps (St. Paul: Christian University Press, 1987), 167. Hatch would not use these ideas to reject thinking and learning.

5. Ibid., 168.

6. C. S. Lewis, "Learning in War-Time," in *The Weight of Glory and Other Addresses* (Grand Rapids: Eerdmans, 1965), 44. Lewis would not have used this point to reject the legitimacy of the life of the mind.

7. Harold Heie, "Integration and Conversation," in *The University through the Eyes of Faith,* ed. Steve Moore (Indianapolis: Light and Life Communications, 1998), 65.

8. Søren Kierkegaard, *Concluding Unscientific Postscript,* trans. Howard V. Hong and Edna H. Hong (Princeton: Princeton University Press, 1992), 132.

9. Ibid., 43.

10. Ibid., 29.

CHAPTER 5 IS THE LIFE OF THE MIND AT ODDS WITH CULTURE?

1. Plato, *The Republic,* trans. Francis M. Cornford (New York: Oxford University Press, 1945), 199, 492B.

2. Aristotle, *Nicomachean Ethics,* trans. Terence Irwin (Indianapolis: Hackett Publishing, 1985), 17 (1098a19).

CHAPTER 6 THE CROWD AND THE COMMUNITY

1. Arthur F. Holmes, *The Soul of the Christian University* (Grand Rapids: Calvin College, 1997), 34.

2. The gracefully written novels of Chaim Potok display this tension poignantly: *The Chosen, The Promise, My Name Is Asher Lev, The Gift of Asher Lev.*

CHAPTER 7 THE HERMIT AND THE EXPLORER

1. Wendell Berry, "The Boundary," in *The Wild Birds: Six Stories of the Port William Membership* (New York: North Point Press, 1986), 81–82.

FURTHER READING

Blamires, Harry. *The Christian Mind: How Should a Christian Think?* Ann Arbor, Mich.: Servant Books, 1978.

Dockery, David S., and David P. Gushee, eds. *The Future of Christian Higher Education.* Nashville: Broadman and Holman, 1999.

Holmes, Arthur. *The Idea of a Christian College.* Rev. ed. Grand Rapids: Eerdmans, 1987.

Marsden, George. *The Outrageous Idea of Christian Scholarship.* New York: Oxford University Press, 1997.

Moreland, J. P. *Love Your God with All Your Mind: The Role of Reason in the Life of the Soul.* Colorado Springs: Navpress, 1997.

Newman, John Henry. *The Idea of a University.* Notre Dame: University of Notre Dame Press, 1982.

Noll, Mark. *The Scandal of the Evangelical Mind.* Grand Rapids: Eerdmans, 1994.

Sertillanges, A. G. *The Intellectual Life: Its Spirit, Conditions, Methods.* Cork, Ireland: The Mercier Press, 1948.

Sire, James W. *Habits of the Mind: Intellectual Life as a Christian Calling.* Downers Grove, Ill.: InterVarsity Press, 2000.

Stott, John R. W. *Your Mind Matters.* Downers Grove, Ill.: InterVarsity Press, 1972.

Trueblood, D. Elton. *The Idea of a College.* New York: Harper & Row, 1959.

Van Doren, Mark. *Liberal Education.* Boston: Beacon Press, 1959.

Clifford Williams (Ph.D., Indiana University) has taught philosophy at Trinity College in Deerfield, Illinois, since 1982. His works include *With All That We Have—Why Aren't We Satisfied?* and *Singleness of Heart: Restoring the Divided Soul.*